Scams and Sweeteners

JAPANESE SOCIETY SERIES

General Editor: Yoshio Sugimoto

Lives of Young Koreans in Japan
Yasunori Fukuoka

Globalization and Social Change in Contemporary Japan
J.S. Eades, Tom Gill and Harumi Befu

Coming Out in Japan: The Story of Satoru and Ryuta
Satoru Ito and Ryuta Yanase

Japan and Its Others:
Globalization, Difference and the Critique of Modernity
John Clammer

Hegemony of Homogeneity:
An Anthropological Analysis of Nihonjinron
Harumi Befu

Foreign Migrants in Contemporary Japan
Hiroshi Komai

A Social History of Science and Technology in
Contempory Japan, Volume 1
Shigeru Nakayama

Farewell to Nippon: Japanese Lifestyle Migrants in Australia
Machiko Sato

The Peripheral Centre:
Essays on Japanese History and Civilization
Johann P. Arnason

A Genealogy of 'Japanese' Self-images
Eiji Oguma

Class Structure in Contemporary Japan
Kenji Hashimoto

An Ecological View of History
Tadao Umesao

Nationalism and Gender
Chizuko Ueno

Native Anthropology: The Japanese Challenge
to Western Academic Hegemony
Takami Kuwayama

Youth Deviance in Japan: Class Reproduction of Non-Conformity
Robert Stuart Yoder

Japanese Companies: Theories and Realities
Masami Nomura and Yoshihiko Kamii

From Salvation to Spirituality:
Popular Religious Movements in Modern Japan
Susumu Shimazono

The 'Big Bang' in Japanese Higher Education: The 2004 Reforms and the Dynamics of Change
J.S. Eades, Roger Goodman and Yumiko Hada

Japanese Politics: An Introduction
Takashi Inoguchi

A Social History of Science and Technology in Contempory Japan, Volume 2
Shigeru Nakayama

Gender and Japanese Management
Kimiko Kimoto

Philosophy of Agricultural Science: A Japanese Perspective
Osamu Soda

A Social History of Science and Technology in Contempory Japan, Volume 3
Shigeru Nakayama and Kunio Goto

Japan's Underclass: Day Laborers and the Homeless
Hideo Aoki

A Social History of Science and Technology in Contemporary Japan, Volume 4
Shigeru Nakayama and Hitoshi Yoshioka

Escape from Work: A Lifestyle Choice of Japanese Youth
Reiko Kosugi

Social Welfare in Japan: Principles and Applications
Kojun Furukawa

Scams and Sweeteners: A Sociology of Fraud
Masahiro Ogino

Social Stratification and Inequality Series

Inequality amid Affluence: Social Stratification in Japan
Junsuke Hara and Kazuo Seiyama

Intentional Social Change: A Rational Choice Theory
Yoshimichi Sato

Constructing Civil Society in Japan: Voices of Environmental Movements
Koichi Hasegawa

Deciphering Stratification and Inequality: Japan and beyond
Yoshimichi Sato

Social Justice in Japan: Concepts, Theories and Paradigms
Ken-ichi Ohbuchi

Advanced Social Research Series

A Sociology of Happiness
Kenji Kosaka

Frontiers of Social Research: Japan and beyond
Akira Furukawa

MODERNITY AND IDENTITY IN ASIA SERIES

Globalization, Culture and Inequality in Asia
Timothy S. Scrase, Todd Miles Joseph Holden and Scott Baum

Looking for Money:
Capitalism and Modernity in an Orang Asli Village
Alberto Gomes

Governance and Democracy in Asia
Takashi Inoguchi and Matthew Carlson

Scams and Sweeteners

A Sociology of Fraud

Masahiro Ogino

Translated by

Lotte Lawrence

Trans Pacific Press

Melbourne

First published in Japanese in 2005 by Sekai Shisōsha as *Reido no shakai: Sagi to zōyo no shakaigaku*

This English language edition published in 2007 by
Trans Pacific Press, PO Box 120, Rosanna, Melbourne, Victoria 3084, Australia
Telephone: +61 3 9459 3021 Fax: +61 3 9457 5923
Email: info@transpacificpress.com
Web: http://www.transpacificpress.com

Designed and set by digital environs, Melbourne. www.digitalenvirons.com

Printed by BPA Print Group, Burwood, Victoria, Australia

Distributors

Australia and New Zealand
UNIREPS
University of New South Wales
Sydney, NSW 2052
Australia
Telephone: +61(0)2-9664-0999
Fax: +61(0)2-9664-5420
Email: info.press@unsw.edu.au
Web: http://www.unireps.com.au

USA and Canada
International Specialized Book
Services (ISBS)
920 NE 58th Avenue, Suite 300
Portland, Oregon 97213-3786
USA
Telephone: (800) 944-6190
Fax: (503) 280-8832
Email: orders@isbs.com
Web: http://www.isbs.com

Asia and the Pacific
Kinokuniya Company Ltd.

Head office:
Shin-Mizonokuchi Bldg. 2F
5-7 Hisamoto 3-chome
Takatsu-ku, Kawasaki 213-8506
Japan
Telephone: +81(0)44-874-9642
Fax: +81(0)44-829-1025
Email: bkimp@kinokuniya.co.jp
Web: www.kinokuniya.co.jp

Asia-Pacific office:
Kinokuniya Book Stores of Singapore Pte., Ltd.
391B Orchard Road #13-06/07/08
Ngee Ann City Tower B
Singapore 238874
Telephone: +65 6276 5558
Fax: +65 6276 5570
Email: SSO@kinokuniya.co.jp

ISSN 1443–9670 (Japanese Society Series)

ISBN 978-1-876843-33-5 (Hardcover)
ISBN 978-1-876843-39-7 (Paperback)

Cover illustration: A scene from an early 18th century *bunraku* puppet play titled *Sonezaki Shinjū* (*The Love Suicides at Sonezaki*), about a man and a woman who fall in love and then commit double suicide after the man becomes the victim of a scam and yet finds himself accused of being the perpetrator.

Contents

Preface ix

1 Exchange and Justice 1
2 Degree-zero Sociality 21
3 Society's Violence 39
4 The Natural State or Sociality at a Standstill 56
5 The Intention to Give Gifts 74
6 The Ambiguous Other 96

Notes 115
Bibliography 117
Index 122

Preface

> Know – if you have a friend in whom you have sure confidence and wish to make use of him, you ought to exchange ideas and gifts with him and go to see him often. If you have another in whom you have no confidence and yet will make use of him, you ought to address him with fair words but crafty heart and repay treachery with lies (Mauss 1969: xiv).

These words were spoken by the most powerful of gods Odin to the troubadour Loddfafnir in the Norse myth *Edda*. Marcel Mauss quotes this passage at the beginning of *The Gift*, Mauss' sociological study of gift-giving. For Mauss, analyzing the act of gift-giving represented a fundamental issue in questioning the principles of society.

I call on the reader to read this quote carefully once again. Another theme lies hidden in this quote that requires addressing by a sociologist. According to Odin, gifts should only be given to friends who can be trusted. This passage was the trigger for Mauss to embark on extensive sociological research on gift-giving. Odin then says that one should only *pretend* to give to those who can not be trusted. This represents something that is as equally important as gift-giving. The word Mauss used, referring to the French translation, is 'dol' or scam. In this book, I have attempted to consider the principles that underlie society through an analysis of scams, just as Mauss used gift-giving as the key term for developing his social theory.

I first developed an interest in scams when I began writing a thesis on the development of capitalism at a university in Paris. An examination of capitalism inevitably leads to an examination of scams. An example is *Sonezaki Shinjū (The Love Suicides at Sonezaki)*, a play written at the beginning of the 18th century by Chikamatsu Monzaemon about a man and a woman who fall in love and commit double suicide. It was not just that their love was an impossible love that triggered the couple's suicide – the main reason was that the male protagonist became a victim of a scam and yet was himself accused of being a scam artist. The economy was booming in the merchant town of Osaka in which the play is set and scams would have been common at the time.

Today, too, countless scams and fraudulent activities continue to be perpetrated. The following is one example that occurred soon after the convenience store near the apartment building where I live closed down. The store had been vacant for some time, when one day a long queue appeared in front of the store. I glanced at a flier inserted into my newspaper that was advertising two kilograms of rice for 100 yen. A store called 'H' had opened and it was holding a 100 yen sale. Chairs lined the inside of the store and customers were invited to sit and listen to a 'beneficial talk' about health and fitness. The real aim, however, was to sell fitness equipment after the talk. Obviously this equipment cost more than 100 yen. The store was located near a nursing home, while elderly people also lived in the nearby housing estate. At the end of the talk, it was these elderly people who found themselves being sold expensive health equipment.

Another example is an incident that I personally experienced. While writing my thesis at a University in Paris I was also regularly interpreting for a Japanese art gallery and even bought large numbers of works by Japanese printmakers at auction. One day we heard that someone living in Geneva, Switzerland, wanted to sell a painting by Gauguin from his 'Tahiti period' and it was quickly decided that the art gallery owner, director and I would go to Geneva. The price of the painting was the equivalent of 3 billion yen (US$25 million), and the gallery owner had brought three cheques made out in American dollars. The offer had been made by a French woman who was not a dealer.

Works from Gauguin's Tahiti period rarely come onto the market and this is what distinguishes Gauguin from other artists such as Renoir who left behind many paintings. I have seen Renoir's work on a number of occasions, and one of these, *Young Girl in a Straw Hat*, is in the private collection of Mr G, the owner of a well-known publishing company who lives in an apartment behind the Church of St Germain de Pres in Paris. Incidentally, wealthy French people (the bourgeoisie) are able to support themselves financially by simply selling a painting in their possession. I clearly remember the strange interior of Mr G's home, which featured an altar in every room.

When I went to Geneva to purchase the Gauguin, I also went to have a look at the Renoir paintings that had been seized by a Swiss bank. A painting from Renoir's *Young Girl in a Straw Hat* series – an example of which I'd seen at Mr G's home – lay on the floor inside one of the enormous safes in the bank. In this example, however, one of the girl's eyes was scratched, and the director of the gallery complained that it had probably been deliberately done by a child.

Back to the story of the Gauguin painting. The French go-between stipulated where the negotiations with 'the vendor' would take place. Before going to the promised location, the gallery owner said half-jokingly that if it was a scam he may as well throw himself into the lake. We happened to be staying at a luxury hotel on the shores of Lake Leman, and we discussed how the three cheques would be handled. Should they be placed in the care of the hotel? No, we couldn't trust the hotel. What about keeping them until we got to the promised location? But what if the vendor was a gangster and we were intimidated into handing over the cheques? In the end it was decided that the gallery owner, the director and I would carry one cheque each to the meeting place.

However, only the go-between was waiting for us at the designated meeting place. The Swiss art dealer, who apparently knew the owner of the painting, was absent. We first told the go-between that a decision could not be made until we saw the actual painting. The go-between contacted the owner and conveyed our message and we were told that the painting could not be shown to us now but that we would be contacted at the hotel as soon as this was possible. We went back to the hotel and sat in our hotel room all day waiting by the telephone. The phone never rang and it was then that we realized that the story about the Gauguin painting was a lie.

Let us return to the story of *Edda*. Mauss is quoting from 'Odin's Warning' in *Edda*. As I mentioned at the beginning, Odin is the highest and most supreme deity in Norse mythology and his warning was recorded by the troubador Loddfafnir. The lexical meaning Loddfafnir means 'one who obtains through deception.' Loddfafnir is, in a word, a 'conman'. In other words, the warning by Odin, the highest and most supreme deity, was conveyed by a conman. If Loddfafnir was nothing more than a conman, the authenticity of Odin's warning can be thrown into doubt. In other words it is possible that the very myth providing the grounds for society was, in fact, nothing but a lie perpetrated by a conman called Loddfafnir.

Myths are simply stories created, once society has been established, in order to indicate the validity of that society. Myths are simply vehicles for policymakers to use the names of gods to authorize their policies. The idea of revealing the fallacy of myths is a characteristic of contemporary thought and sociology is no exception. The sociologist has used various conceptual devices to convey 'contrivance' and 'fallacy.' The aim of this book, however, is not simply to repeat the sociologist's thoughts to date on the subject but also to reveal the fraudulent nature of society itself. What I would like to consider, using the word 'scam' or 'fraud', is the 'blank space' found in society. Accepted social norms do not penetrate every corner of society. There are always 'blank spaces', social fissures in which such norms do not apply. As we saw earlier, the long queue that suddenly appeared at the 100 yen sale appears in such social fissures. Alternatively, it is this queue itself that creates a blank space in society. The Swiss scam artist who never appeared also dwells in this blank space. Social norms do not apply here. In society's blank spaces one must make a decision in response to each situation that arises.

It is these blank spaces in society that enable scams to take place. These places represent a world filled with uncertainty and where at times violence erupts. Because of the absence of clear norms it also enables the establishment of uninhibited relationships. The departure point for this book poses the possibility that it is this world of blank spaces which is in fact the 'primary world.'

In the sense that norms do not apply in the world of blank spaces, such a world is a world of degree-zero sociality. However, here lies a 'society' that is different from one controlled by norms. It represents another way of survival that can be described as degree-zero society. Society that is controlled by standards is a dangerous and fragile world situated at ground zero. Like Cambodia under the control of the Pol Pot regime, a society that attempts to eliminate every type of blank space or fissure and forces the citizens to conform to national norms, in the end, meets its downfall.

Unlike Odin's warning, there is no clear delineation between friendship and respect, and gift-giving and scams, in degree-zero society. There is no differentiation between a premeditated scam and the intention to give a gift, and one could easily become the other, so that a situation may seem like a scam but could equally seem like an example of gift-giving. There is a need for a sociological theory focusing on a primordial world where no differentiation can be made between a scam or a pure act of giving: a world of degree-zero sociality.

1 Exchange and Justice

The birth of individualism

In everyday situations, we make a decision as to whether something is right or wrong. For example, when trying to arrive at destination A, there is 'the right way' for one to get there. Even if it were a detour, it would still be 'the right way' as long as we arrived at A.

The reason we are able to arrive at A is because we knew the right way to get there. In other words, the decision of whether something is right or wrong depends on whether we have the correct knowledge or information at hand. If it is a geographical destination such as a café located in front of the train station which two people designate as a meeting place, deciding on the right way to get there would be simple. Getting to the café successfully proves that we used the right information to do so.

However it is not always easy to determine what is right and it can often be very difficult. Science involves addressing issues in which what is right or wrong remains unknown and the research that is constantly carried out to identify what information is correct is a never-ending process. This is because, in science, even if the perfect knowledge were to exist to enable what is right to be determined, it is something that can only be attained over time.

Religion and philosophy attempt to teach us to identify what is right. Even then, however, we do not know exactly what is right or not. Theological debate is generated as a result of differing opinions on the interpretation of Holy Scriptures and this in itself conveys the fact that what is right has not been fully determined. Meanwhile, ethics involves endless discussions on what is right or not, and this in itself conveys that we do not actually know what is right or true.

This applies not only to science or religion but also to our everyday lives. Our actions are based on decisions of whether something is 'right', without really knowing what that may be. In many cases the rules for making these decisions already exist and we simply act in accordance with these rules. We do not, however, go to the trouble of questioning whether these rules are correct. To question the effectiveness of rules remains the role of science or religion.

Rules include laws regulating natural phenomena through to laws regulating human action. This book addresses the latter, and there are two perspectives that can be taken. One is to seek the rationale for these laws in a nonhuman and transcendental being. In this case, the transcendental being would either be a god or a specific State. However, as expressed by the proverb 'When in Rome, do as the Romans do', because of the empirical fact that rules can change depending on the location, and therefore the transcendental being which represents the rationale for the rules can also change, we must assume that a universal god or State applicable to all places simply does not exist. The countless religious wars that have been fought throughout history have taught us that when people are forced to worship a specific god there will always be those who reject such attempts.

Is there an alternative perspective? This would obviously be to seek the rationale for rules in the very people that created those rules. A typical line of thought is to seek the rationale for justice in 'justice in exchange' (Takeuchi 2002). Let us call this the 'market principle.' The reason I have used this term is because this debate is based on the topic of market exchange. In the market principle, a just exchange represents equal exchange between two parties. The argument for punishing acts that involve selling something that is almost worthless for profit, or not repaying borrowed money, or fraud or embezzlement, is that punishment restores justice. The market principalist believes that people have a propensity for exchange, and moreover, that the exchange that is carried out must be at the normal price. This is conveyed simply by Adam Smith's statement that 'If among a nation of hunters, for example, it usually costs twice the labour to kill a beaver which it does to kill a deer, one beaver should naturally exchange for or be worth two deer' (Smith 1986: 150). Using the example that hunting people 'in barbarous and uncivilized states' carried out exchange, Smith argues that people have a natural tendency to carry out exchange. This exchange, however, must be equivalent. That this is raised by Smith implies that there is a possibility that the exchange might not be equivalent. Therefore exchange that is not equivalent is wrong and therefore must be punished. This is the market principalist's view of justice.

The market principalist is an individualist in every way. To the individualist, people make logical decisions based on their own standards. People are essentially self-reliant and have been as far back as the 'barbarous and uncivilized' hunting peoples. This is conveyed by Smith's observation that equivalent exchange is carried out by hunting people in which hunters assess the value of their prey and then carry out an exchange of equivalent value.

However, from the argument developed by Marcel Mauss in *The Gift* and from the results of economic anthropology research that has been carried out by Karl Polanyi (Polanyi 1957) and researchers since, we now know that it is questionable whether 'uncivilized people' were in fact individualists. Mauss' theory on gift-giving points out that the exchange of items is not carried out between individuals but between collectives, and that the items of exchange are not everyday items. 'Uncivilized people' do not necessarily assess the value of each others' 'products' when bartering. This is because gift-giving is also incorporated into the act of exchange and is based on a logic that is different from that of market economics. As the theory of gift-giving is discussed in further detail in chapter 5, let us now consider the issue of individualism.

Smith saw market theory as operating in all societies and saw individualism as something universal that is found in every society. This, however, is nothing more than a myth generated in a society in which the market principle, which Smith saw as ideal, had already been established. I am definitely an individual with the name Masahiro Ogino. However, this is because the system recognizes me as Masahiro Ogino.

My first name Masahiro was given to me by my parents at my birth and was notified to the local ward office. The simple reference that differentiates me from others was selected and acknowledged by those other than myself. This is the name that I was referred to at kindergarten and primary school. At some stage I became aware of the fact that my name was Masahiro Ogino, so that if someone called out the words 'Masahiro Ogino' I would immediately respond. I have no problems whatsoever in identifying myself as Masahiro Ogino. As long as I am living in this society, Masahiro Ogino is what differentiates me from others and is the simplest reference to convey my existence. When a book that I write is published, the author Masahiro Ogino's name appears on the cover together with the title.

This represents the varied process in which the individual is created that includes the name given to the individual and what the individual is called by others (Althusser 1970). The awareness that I am not a stranger, that I am nothing other than myself, is generated by the existence of others. Therefore, arguably, the awareness of being an individual is something that develops when a specific 'place' in society is allocated to that individual. In this case, to be an individual means to become a member of society by identifying with society's norms. An individual can only exist as part of society. According to Bulgarian writer Elias Canetti,

> Men as individuals are always conscious of these distinctions; they weigh heavily on them and keep them firmly apart from one another. (abbreviated) Only together can men free themselves from their burdens of distance (Canetti 1978: 17–18).

Canetti describes the individual as nothing more than a representation of the disparities between people, which differs from the market principalists' perception of the individual. This is because the market principalist does not perceive the individual as an inherent part of society but as existing independently from society. According to anthropologist Louis Dumont, this particular view, i.e. individualism, emerged in the West during the 17th Century. It was Adam Smith's philosophy that heralded the arrival of this individualist society (Dumont 1977)[1].

The emergence of this society was triggered by a view of the individual as one who is not economically reliant on others and has the ability to be self-supporting. For example, 17th Century political philosopher John Locke's view of the individual was one who produced goods and built wealth through his own labor (Locke 1947). Therefore, as long as I continue to be financially supported by my parents I am not, wholly, an individual. Unless I can carry out independent and productive activity using my own resources, I am not, strictly speaking, seen as an individual. An individual, both in name and in reality, is an adult who owns property and who can survive on one's own without depending on others. Locke, believing that human free will is supported by an individual's powers of understanding, made the following statement:

> … wherein he has not *Understanding* of his own to direct his *Will*, he is not to have any Will of his own to follow; He that *understands* for him, must *will* for him too; he must prescribe to his Will, and regulate his Actions: but when he comes to the Estate that made his *Father a Freeman*, the *Son is a Freeman* too (Locke 1947: 324–5).

Locke discusses the duties of a parent towards the child. Although God has endowed humans with 'the freedom to will and the freedom of action', we are unable to fully enjoy this freedom while we are still children.

If, therefore, an individual is an adult who owns property, in reality there would have been countless numbers of people who could never be wholly independent. Those who are unable to become independent are therefore not wholly individuals[2]. To make a name for oneself as an individual means to own property in one's namc, and not everyone can become individuals. This is clearly conveyed through the history of popular suffrage. For many years, only males with a certain level of assets (paying a certain level of taxes) had the right to vote. If one had no personal assets, one did not have the right of an individual to express one's political opinion.

Locke refers to the issue of the large numbers of people who were not able to become independent or, in other words, did not have assets, and discussed measures to overcome this problem (Locke 1947). Locke examines poverty as the reason for the inability of people to become independent and divides the poor into three categories. The first category represents those who required assistance such as the disabled. The second category represents those who had worked in the past but who now required assistance, a typical example of which would be the elderly. The third category represents the able-bodied who required assistance and this category is divided into those who have jobs but are unable to support their families and those without jobs, that is, the unemployed. To address the unemployed group in particular, Locke proposes the utilization of the textile industry and the establishment of schools (working schools) for the children of poor families.

It was during the 18th Century that, based on Locke's philosophy, those who did not own assets began to be seen as individuals. According to Michel Foucault, 'In a system of discipline, the child is more individualized than the adult, the patient more than the healthy man, the madman and the delinquent more than the normal and the non-delinquent' (Foucault 1979: 193). In Foucault's disciplinary system, those who are disciplined (children or criminals) are seen as 'individuals' and continue to be monitored. This involves body checks and various 'tests' to record the characteristics of the individual. Society establishes people as individuals by keeping them captive, disciplined and tamed.

In this way, once into the 19th Century, a system developed in which the dominant norm was the economically self-reliant individual who adhered to a set of rules and a moral code that taught not to encroach on others' assets. Meanwhile, those without any personal assets were imparted assets by society and were developed into proprietors = individuals. In other words society began to assist individuals who were unable to become autonomous.

Foucault's view of the individual differs slightly from that of Dumont. Dumont's individualist ideology saw the individual as being a subject who asserts a will. In contrast, Foucault's individual is nothing more than the smallest unit necessary for authorities to carry out effective control, and there is no particular emphasis on the individual as an autonomous presence. This difference in perception lies in the fact that unlike Dumont, who sees the owner, or the bourgeois, as the model for the individual, Foucault sees those who do not own, in particular laborers, as individuals. In other words, the difference between Foucault and Dumont depends on which of the two classes that form capitalist society the debate should be based on and developed.

Regardless of this difference, however, one aspect of capitalist society is addressed in both Foucault and Dumont's theories. This is the social recording of the individual in various ways. When the individual owns assets, this means that the land is registered under the individual's name, a savings account opened, and shares bought and sold in that individual's name. Meanwhile, children and 'the abnormal' are detained in schools, prisons, hospitals and factories and rigorous records of these people, as individuals, are maintained in these institutions.

As a result the individual or 'I' is seen as uniform. This is why, in an individualist society, the definition of someone who is independent of society is examined. In contrast, if the individual is an integral part of society, to what extent that individual is consistent with the definition of an individual is not greatly emphasized. If anything, the emphasis is on the changes that take place at various stages of the individual's life, with these stages being celebrated. A rite of passage, for example, is of great importance in society. It is by passing through these rites of passage that one becomes a so-called member of society.

The scam as part of the exchange

Since the 17th Century, the individual in Western Europe has been viewed as nothing more than a 'product.' Having said this, in an individualist society everybody 'becomes' an individual. However, whether a smooth and equivalent exchange was carried out by every person in an individualist society is debatable. This is because irregularities and scams are associated with any exchange.

The popularization of the commodity economy was frequently accompanied by scams. As an example, *Sonezaki Shinjū* [The Love Suicides at Sonezaki] – the first work in Chikamatsu Monzaemon's *Sewamono* and first performed in 1703 – is about the double suicide of the courtesan Ohatsu and Tokubei. The catalyst for the suicide was Tokubei being tricked out of his money by Kuheiji whom Tokubei had believed was a friend. Kuheiji's skilful manipulation of the situation resulted in Tokubei being accused as the perpetrator of the scam. In other words, the scam is an important element of the storyline in *Sonezaki Shinjū* and indicates how scams and fraud were already recognized as such by Chikamatsu and the merchants of Osaka and how there were no effective measures to address these incidents at the time (Ogino 1998: 26–69). *Sonezaki Shinjū* is set in 18th Century Osaka, a city where the commodity economy was rapidly developing, but in which a system to regulate fraud and scams was yet to be established. In such an environment, those unaccustomed to the commodity economy would have soon found themselves victims of conmen and scam artists.

Tsuneichi Miyamoto, listening to the story told to him by one Sakon Kumata makes the following observation about rural communities during the early Meiji period.

> In his youth, Sakon also lived in a world in which it was not possible to distinguish between rumors and truth. In such a situation, you could not live by being suspicious of others. Once you became suspicious then there would be no end to it. Once deceived, you could never trust anyone else again. Although being illiterate meant that life was almost ridiculously carefree, Sakon did his best to not trust strangers (Miyamoto 1984: 251–2).

The world that illiterate people lived in was a world in which people 'were unable to distinguish between what was true and what was not' (Miyamoto [1960]1984: 249). These people lived in a different dimension from those who were able to decide on what was true or false. Even after the introduction of contracts, legal systems and the commodity economy, illiterate people remained powerless and were easy victims of conmen and scam artists. As the majority of villagers were illiterate, the losses suffered were unfathomable' (Miyamoto 1984: 247).

With the development of capitalism, the market principalist's sense of justice began to be accepted and at the same time there was a growing clampdown on scams. Fraud legislation came into effect in England during the 18th Century. The 1799 Statute related to embezzlement, punishing for example clerks who pocketed money received from customers, was enacted in 1799 after an incident (the Bazely Case) in which a bank cashier who pocketed a certificate was found not guilty as no law existed at the time to punish such an act (Kimura 2000: 73). Fraud was established as a criminal act for the first time in Germany with the 1851 Prussian Criminal Code 241 (Kimura 2000: 12). In other words, the more capitalism developed the greater the recognition of fraudulent acts and the more it was legislated.

The justice of market economics was, however, not recognized in villages where the commodity economy was unfamiliar. Justice is not determined by whether an exchange is equivalent or not. A sense of justice in reference to an act of exchange emerged with the development of the commodity economy while there was a greater recognition of the potential for scams. As people began to accumulate assets, those favoring the individualism-based exchange of equivalents began to become fearful of somehow losing their assets or of being defrauded. Descartes' famous *Discours de la Methode* hints at this. According to Descartes, in order to live a stable and secure life, it is important to acquire skills that enable one to verify whether something is true or not, and that in the pursuit of truth one must read books and travel. According to Descartes, 'I had always had an extreme desire to learn to distinguish true from false in order to see clearly into my own actions and to walk with safety in this life' (Descartes 1968). In reality, however, nothing convinced Descartes. Even philosophy, which initially appears to be theorizing truth, in fact only presents a pretend truth. Finally, after doubting everything, Descartes arrived at the 'truth' that the doubting self can not be doubted, resulting in the famous quote 'I think, therefore I am.'

Descartes' philosophy places the 'I' as the standard for making decisions. I am an autonomous being who can rigorously differentiate between what is true and false. This is the philosophy of individualism and at the same time the philosophy of anti-fraud. It was Descartes' pursuit of certainty and his fear and insecurity of being deceived by others that propelled him to shape his view of people as individuals with a consistent will to be autonomous.

Certainty in life means the following:

1. The certainty that one's own labor creates wealth
2. The certainty, when selling excess products, of being paid an appropriate consideration

In the case of (1), although it may seem that scams are not possible when labor involves the individual cultivation of land, unless the person is totally isolated, there is always the danger of the land being misappropriated by an outsider. The danger is even greater in (2). This is because it is difficult to decide whether the return is equivalent or more than the equal value, and therefore there is the constant danger of being defrauded.

The deceiver and the deceived

George Simmel was the first sociologist to become aware of the importance of fraud. According to Simmel, because one can never completely know what another is thinking, the truth can be conveyed but it is equally possible to deceive (Simmel 1908). Simmel also points out that people often have to deceive others in order to survive while some even choose to be deceived. According to this view, fraud or scams constantly lurk at the foundation of human relationships.

According to Simmel, there is a likelihood of fraud being perpetrated during an exchange of products when there is a significant disparity in the knowledge of the product between the vendor and the purchaser. The purchaser's knowledge of the product is considerably inferior in comparison to the vendor's. Therefore, there is the possibility of the purchaser being deceived by the vendor. This is not restricted to commercial transactions. Conversations are conducted without either party carrying out a detailed check on whether what the other is saying is true or not. In actual fact, if the details of a conversation were checked each time one party said something, there would probably be no conversation. The reality therefore is that, at times, one can be deceived by another. Scams are a danger that inevitably accompanies communication.

The symbolic interaction theorists who were in no small part influenced by Simmel share a similar view on fraud and scams. For example, symbolic interaction theorists believe that fraud is generated by a difference in the level of information about a situation and the ability to manipulate that information (Katagiri 1996). A conman who attempts to sell imitation jewelry pretends to be a jewelry dealer, acting as though the transaction was authentic. The person being deceived believes that the situation created by the conman is authentic and is unaware of the trap that has been set. Information can be manipulated in a transaction when one party has significantly less information than the other and it is in such situations that one can end up being deceived.

The symbolic interaction theorists emphasize that acting appropriately in a specific situation results in interaction. Whether a performance is real or not is not the issue. If one can act appropriately as the occasion arises, interaction will take place. All that is required in interaction is for both parties to carry out what appears to be the appropriate performance in relation to each other. The conman maximizes the performance characteristics of interaction to get the other person to buy the imitation.

However, it is not enough for the conman to be superior to the other party in terms of information and knowledge and to have the skills to actively create the 'secret.' Simply pointing out the uncertainty that lies between the conman and the victim does not clarify its meaning. One point that can be raised here is that people are not simply passive victims of a conman and in some cases actually choose to be deceived. In Thomas Mann's novel *Confessions of Felix Krull*, Krull describes his desire to be seduced or, more to the point, deceived as 'a general human need, implanted by God Himself in human nature' (Mann 1958: 28). According to Krull, people are not deceived simply because they are ignorant but at times are happily deceived. Although Simmel touches on this point, the focus of his argument lies in the difference in the level of information between two parties during communication.

Let us now examine the characteristics of scams and the characteristics of communication itself which was overlooked by Simmel and the symbolic interaction theorists by examining the Ashikaga Bank Embezzlement that was uncovered in 1975.

On 11 August 1973, Akiko Ōbayashi (pseudonym), a loan officer at the Tochigi Branch of the Ashikaga Branch (age 21 at the time) was on a train heading for Sendai where she happened to meet a man who described himself as 'an international secret service agent in pursuit of Gorgo 13.' Ōbayashi did not question the man's words, related to him as though he really was a secret service agent and immediately and with no hesitation became involved with him. The man gave his name as Masayuki Abe (pseudonym) (age 23 at the time). Ten days after they met, Abe asked Ōbayashi for a loan, telling her that he needed funds to enable him to leave the international secret police organization. Ōbayashi initially gave Abe 600,000 yen (US$5,000) from her father's savings and then another 700,000 yen (US$5,800) from her father's and her own savings. The third and subsequent times, Ōbayashi fabricated loan documents and over a period of approximately two years she withdrew, on 53 occasions, funds totaling 200 million yen (US$1.7 million) from the Ashikaga Bank (Yamazaki & Serizawa, 1989: 61).

Relationships in scams are generally formed spontaneously. The other party does not suspect the conman's words and believes everything they are told. Alternatively, and more accurately, the relationship is formed in a place in which the issue of trust or faith – believing or not believing – can not addressed. Such a relationship is formed by what can only be described as a certain 'energy' emitted by the conman, and this relationship continues until the intervention by a third party. This is because the conman's secret is only revealed with the intervention of a third party, which results in the revelation of the scam. At every stage before this revelation, that is, while the deceiver and the deceived are joined in complicity, whether one is being secretive or not is not an issue. It is a relationship that transcends differences in the level of information between the two parties. It is a fundamental relationship that exists even before the intervention of words.

Until the very end, Ōbayashi did not know Abe's real name or where he lived. Abe used a different name – Ishimura, Okamoto and Shiratori, amongst others – each time he saw Ōbayashi. When Ōbayashi's forged promissory notes were uncovered and the Tochigi Prefectural Police began investigating the matter, the police found it difficult to believe Ōbayashi's statement that she knew nothing about her accomplice Abe. As a result, Abe managed to escape arrest even after police dispatched six unmarked police cars to the location where Ōbayashi had promised to meet Abe. Names and addresses were of no importance to Ōbayashi and Abe.

Kazuhisa Nishihara reflects Alfred Schutz's views when he describes the relationship formed by two people who are mutually 'tuning-in' to each other as a 'mutual tuning-in relationship' (Nishihara 2003: 78). This mutual tuning-in relationship had clearly been established between Ōbayashi and Abe. Ōbayashi had effortlessly tuned into Abe without or before questioning who he really was.

An inherent beat resonates when two people are tuned in to each other. Schutz cites the example of a musical performance as a typical mutual tuning-in relationship, in particular a string quartet which in fact is a form of music that has already been socially systematized. The relationship between a conman and the person being deceived is significantly more mutually tuned-in than a music performance, the prerequisite of which is the presence of an audience. This is because the relationship is suddenly formed without any concerns as to whom the other person is. It can only be described as a relationship that marches to its own beat. In this relationship neither the con artist nor the person being conned sees the other within a social context. The experience can be described as a 'pure experience' that exists before any social meaning is applied through words (Fujitani 1999: 78).

This pure experience – defined by William James as the raw reality of a "'pure' state, plain unqualified actuality' (James 1912), in other words the state in which there is no meaning, or the state that exists before meaning, disappears the moment that meaning is applied. In this way, meaning is conferred on every experience. Even fraudulent relationships initially appear the same. However, when Abe introduced himself to Ōbayashi as 'an international secret service agent in pursuit of Gorgo 13', a statement that most people would find preposterous, 'meaning' itself had in fact been destroyed. Once meaning was destroyed, Ōbayashi was able to embark on a totally new adventure. Ōbayashi did not see Abe's description of himself as being preposterous, and was instantly freed from any existing knowledge (which could be described as 'common sense'). The knowledge dictating to her that she should not respond to a strange man approaching her on a train, that a bank teller should never set up a fictitious loan had no meaning to Ōbayashi who instead saw new possibilities and choices.

Ōbayashi continued to give Abe money for two years following their encounter. When Ōbayashi was asked during the trial how she felt when she first gave money to Abe, she replied that she felt sorry about what she had done and did not know why she gave him the money but that she was definitely attracted to him. She also said that even though she'd tell herself that she wouldn't do it again, each time she saw him, for some reason she 'would always end up promising to give him more money' (Sawaji 1976).

Why did Ōbayashi continue to give money to Abe without keeping any of the money for herself? A typical answer would be that it was because he'd promised to marry her. At the trial, however, Ōbayashi said that she had no expectations of marrying Abe. She said only that she was always afraid that he would leave her. According to one account, Ōbayashi had become 'romantically involved with a married man with children from around the end of 1974' (Sawaji 1976), but continued giving money to Abe while remaining involved with the married man. When the crime was revealed, Ōbayashi's immediate reaction was to plead that Abe not be arrested.

However, in court, Abe said that 'You might all think that I feel bad about Ms Ōbayashi but in fact I don't.' He also told the court that he had not 'intimidated or been violent towards Ōbayashi' and in fact seemed almost completely unaware that he had deceived her. This reaction can not be dismissed as Abe simply making excuses.

Something must have prompted Ōbayashi to respond to Abe. One factor would have been Abe's conman personality, something that will be discussed in more detail in the next section. Let us first examine Ōbayashi's situation.

Ōbayashi did well at high school and was an outstanding bank employee and it was because of this that she was trusted by the bank and therefore able to continue to embezzle funds for over two years. Ōbayashi had lost her forefinger as a young child and she recalled being 'constantly teased by boys at kindergarten and primary school and always crying. Shortly before the trip to Sendai (author's note – during which Ōbayashi met Abe), I was told by a colleague that shaking hands with someone without a finger made them feel ill. I knew then that I could never be normal.' Ōbayashi was searching for a way out of this normal world that was so alien to her and to discover a different world, and it was just at that time that the 'international secret service agent' made his appearance.

For Ōbayashi, fabricating a loan so that she could give money to Abe the agent would have seemed more real to her than efficiently carrying out her normal work duties. In one sense this very process was gradually leading her away from the environment of the bank, where all she felt was a sense of alienation, into a different world. It was at this point that Ōbayashi was 'transformed.'

Abe was in fact seeing another woman during the two years that he was obtaining money from Ōbayashi. He first started living in Chiba with a bar hostess whom he met at a bar in Shibuya. Using the funds that he obtained from Ōbayashi, Abe then set up a company called International Union Development Center (pseudonym), employing around 40 staff (refer to chapter 5 for details). Abe went on to marry one of his employees and the wedding was held in Hawaii, paid for by the funds that he obtained from Ōbayashi.

Ōbayashi's embezzlement was discovered by the Ashikaga Bank in 1975. At the time, Abe was seeing a woman called Yukiko Kashimura (pseudonym). Kashimura (who was married) submitted a notification of divorce on the day after a warrant was issued for Abe's arrest. Six days later she discovered that Abe was being pursued by the police. Kashimura chose to go into hiding with Abe and the two began life on the run. The couple went to Kanazawa where they rented an apartment under the guise of a student sitting his university entrance exam and his sister. Kashimura was arrested when she went to a bank to withdraw her savings, while Abe was arrested soon after in Tokyo. Although Kashimura's actions are easier to understand than Ōbayashi's, she is no different from Ōbayashi in the sense she willingly entered Abe's world. In her statement, Kashimura said that 'life was tough but I felt completely fulfilled…I didn't care what happened to me, I just wanted to make sure Abe could avoid arrest for even one more day so that I could be with him for just that much longer' (Sawaji 1976).

Kashimura, too, had been transformed by her encounter with Abe.

The ideal conman

What sort of person is a conman who can bring about such a transformation? I shall first define the essential characteristics of a conman from a philosophical perspective.

The conman abandons his past

As Foucault pointed out, the individual is first recorded at birth when he/she also begins to develop a memory as an individual. The thought of losing one's memory is frightening enough (Hamada 2002). Foucault saw the individual as a prison from which it was difficult to escape, but in his later years discovered several possibilities. One was the 'entitification' seen amongst ancient Greeks. The ancient Greeks continued to carry out entitification by acting out one's life. This, however, was only made possible because of the characteristics of ancient Greek society (Deleuze 1990). The other is 'passion' referred to in Deleuze's conversation with German stage director Werner Schroeter.

> People, when affected by passion, do not necessarily become blinded but they do lose a sense of self (Foucault 1994) .

Passion suddenly attacks people unawares, putting them in a constantly insecure state. It is, however, in this very state that lies the potential to become someone else, to establish a new way of communicating. It is a state that can neither be named nor classified and it is this very state that makes aesthetic interpretation possible.

> The art of living involves the destruction of psychologism and, with others, the creation of originality, existence, relationship and beauty which can not be named (Foucault 1994).

To caution people not to become the victims of a cheap psychologism is extremely important to Foucault. This is because psychologism is nothing more than a product of capitalist society that encourages individualization. From Foucault's perspective, assuming the existence of a consistent self that is central to the individual signifies falling into the trap laid by authority. In order to escape from the trap of individualization, the self must no longer be a self and passion is a way to enable this to take place.

Certainly, passion can be seen as an agent for establishing 'originality' and 'a new way of communicating.' Ōbayashi was controlled by passion. The conman is a director who is able to draw out passion from others.

This is because the conman is the only person who is not preoccupied by the other's past and for whom oblivion represents the primary power. The conman gives his name but it is not his real name. That name is not registered with the authorities or anywhere else. A conman is essentially a drifter, never settling in one place. His movements can therefore not be predicted. Referring to Abe while he was on the run from authorities, one prosecutor made the following statement: 'We would normally have information on persons that a fugitive would clearly want to make contact with, but in this man's case we have no such information' (*Shūkan Shinchō*, 28 August 1975 issue).

The reason the conman's movements can not be predicted is because a conman is the antithesis of the consistent self that is the premise of individualism, and can be described as an 'invert image' of the individual. In order to live as an individual, one must build a history as that individual. However, the conman rejects the very building of a personal history. Resisting the building of a personal history, the conman instead tries to create his own and unique space and time.

The conman does this by prompting a change (= difference). The conman, who does not settle in one place, creates a tiny fissure in spaces such as inside a train. Abe's preposterous claim that he is pursuing Gorgo 13 automatically rejects Ōbayashi, Kashimura or the conman Abe's own pasts and creates a future that is not bound by the past.

The conman is tolerant

The conman who is not preoccupied with the past is obviously not caught up by conventions. Ōbayashi lost the end of her forefinger as a young child and was hurt by a remark by another bank employee who told her that shaking hands with a woman without a finger made him feel ill. Abe, however, did not discriminate against a woman with a missing finger. Abe, so different from the norm and who appeared cavalier and irresponsible in the eyes of others in fact reassured Ōbayashi and enabled her to forget the burden of having a missing finger.

Moreover, Abe was never violent or arrogant towards Ōbayashi. Abe never made Ōbayashi feel beholden to him. Ōbayashi terminated the decision-making process of determining whether she was being deceived by this man, or what this man's true identity was, instead allowing herself to be seduced by Abe and lending or giving him money. It was not simply a case of Ōbayashi not suspecting Abe and gullibly accepting what he told her. She was complicit as she immersed herself in his world.

Ōbayashi herself did not know why she lent money to a man she knew nothing about. However, it was Abe's tolerance which initially appeared as disinterest on his part that attracted Ōbayashi in the first place. This tolerant and non-exclusive attitude represents the second characteristic of the conman. It is directly related to the rejection of 'the recorded.' In order to enable an individual to be recorded, a method of classifying the information to be recorded is first needed. In other words, individualism inevitably classifies and differentiates people. To reject exclusivity represents a rejection of the intention to classify in this way. This persistent tolerance destroys the very inclination to classify people based on certain standards.

The conman gambles on superficial appearances

The conman who attempts to survive in 'the here and now' by rejecting his past is gambling on superficial appearances. This represents the conman's third characteristic and is a familiar view in sociological theory. Symbolic interaction theory emphasizes that all that matters in interaction is that the two parties appear to be performing appropriately in front of each other. This necessitates 'a shared definition of the situation', and a con or scam is enabled when the definition[3] of the situation is conscious.

However, this 'gambling on superficial appearances' is different from this theory. In symbolic interaction theory, it is assumed that the 'performing self' lies behind the 'real self.' This is because of the assumption that a strategic individual performs in response to the situation. However, the conman is not an individual consisting of 'a surface' and 'what lies below the surface', or 'the external' and 'the internal.' For example, Abe approaches Ōbayashi with the 'title' of 'an international secret service agent in pursuit of Gorgo 13.' This claim may seem preposterous, but of importance here is that, behind this title, Abe's 'real face' or his 'real nature' is invisible. The world that Abe creates is a totally superficial world. It represents nothing more than the stage scenery ready for the play he is about to direct. Even his 'character' (if, in fact, this actually exists) is nothing more than a prop.

There is also a difference between this and the argument put forward by Harold Garfinkel who criticized Goffman's concept of self-presentation and instead presented the concept of 'passing.' In his thesis *Passing and the managed achievement of sex status in an intersexed person*, Garfinkel discusses the 36 hours of interviews with Agnes, a 19 year old typist who 'appeared as a person with feminine body contours and hair pattern. She had large, well-developed breasts together with male genitals.' 'Until the age of seventeen she was recognized by everyone as a boy' (Garfinkel 1967: 119–20). When she turned 17, however, she went to 'a city in the Mid-West' where she wore women's clothing and changed her hairstyle. She was then employed as a woman and even had a boyfriend called Bob. However, Bob's demands for sex and marriage began to grow and Agnes finally revealed her 'true situation' to him. Agnes then went to the UCLA (University of California, Los Angeles) Medical Center where she underwent a sex change operation.

According to Garfinkel, Agnes went to great lengths to appear feminine and continues to learn how to behave in order to appear feminine. He then defines passing as follows:

> The work of achieving and making secure her rights to live as a normal, natural female while having continually to provide for the possibility of detection and ruin carried on within socially structured conditions I call Agnes' "passing."' (Garfinkel 1967: 137)

According to Garfinkel, passing is something that 'succeeds' over a long period of time. Simply pointing out 'self-presentation' in a specific setting, that there is an act in response to a situation, as Goffman does, is insufficient.

Agnes' passing is carried out by skillfully concealing her own identity. For example, Agnes had to present a urine sample during the physical examination that was a condition of employment by the insurance company, but had to use the toilet installed in the medical office rather than the normal toilet. A nurse could have walked into the medical office while Agnes was touching genitals. Agnes therefore sat on the toilet, pretending she was urinating, then told the doctor that she couldn't produce a sample and that she would bring one in by the end of the day. She went home to the apartment where her room mate was waiting. Agnes, fearing that the urine test would reveal her gender, told her room mate that she was suffering from a kidney inflammation, that this could show up in her urine and that it could affect her chances of getting the job. Her house mate happily provided her with a urine sample, which Agnes then took to the doctor.

One's identity can certainly be created through a process such as Agnes' passing. However, the premise of passing is that there are two selves – the self that is unknown (and that, if known, would create problems) and the self you want others to identify you with. This indicates that passing itself does not represent a questioning of the existing order but is a process of how best to slot oneself into the existing order. Agnes simply wanted to achieve the status of a woman and totally embraces 'femininity' and 'feminine behavior', the indicators of cultural differentiation.

In contrast, the conman has a cynical view of status. The conman does not worship status. In other words, that he gambles on superficiality signifies that the conman has no interest in achieving status. To the conman the very act of social integration is something intolerable. Rather, the conman is indifferent to social rules and is barely aware of their existence. Therefore, even though the conman may attempt to use rules to control, he would never adhere to the rules themselves. The conman always manages to avoid being controlled by society, no matter how much society attempts to do so. It would be unthinkable for a conman to engage in production through one's labor, and to make a living through one's efforts, while saving money is out of the question. Any funds obtained through a con or scam is soon squandered. The conman therefore never owns assets. In this sense, too, the conman is the extreme opposite of 'the individual.'

There was once a famous conman called Jonaf Elizabeth Kuhio. Kuhio proposed marriage to a young office worker living in Kasukabe City, Saitama Prefecture. He told her that he was a 37 year old US Air Force captain called Jonaf Elizabeth Kuhio, that his mother was the younger sister of Queen Elizabeth and his father a descendant of Hawaii's King Kamehameha and that he had 50 billion yen ($US 42 million) in assets. He told the young woman that he would give her 2 billion yen ($US 1.7 million) as a dowry if she would marry him. The two began living together. One day, Kuhio told her that he'd made a dent in the funds that he was managing at the Yokota Air Base and that he would be court-martialed if this was discovered. He told her that he needed 3 million yen ($US 25,000) to cover his losses and that he would pay her back immediately. In the end Kuhio received a total of 8.5 million yen ($US 71,000) from the woman's older brother (*Shūkan Bunshun*, 8 April 1993 issue).

Kuhio was originally from Hokkaido and rarely held down a job after graduating from high school. If, after becoming an adult, it is one's past that represents one's 'true face', then there was very little of a 'true face' in Kuhio. Kuhio focused only on creating an image, a surface. He had cosmetic surgery on his nose, dyed his hair chestnut brown and wore a military uniform. There was no 'real face' under the surface/mask of a US Air Force pilot. This surface/mask was unique to Kuhio and did not exist anywhere else. Although there were slight changes, such a change in name from 'Prince Jona Kuhio' to Jonaf Elizabeth Kuhio, Kuhio 'repeated' his one identity – that of Kuhio – in approaching several women.

The conman has no interest in social evaluation and creates his 'surface' based on whim. As a result, the conman illuminates the existence of a reality distinct from reality as defined in social science (social reality). The presence of the conman makes it clear that the world consists of two different and overlapping realities. On the one hand there is reality as recognized by society. For obvious reasons, how reality is perceived differs depending on the type of society. In a capitalist society, having a steady job and making an honest living are seen as being realistic. Without these, one is said to 'not know what reality is' or to be 'unrealistic.' There is, however, a reality that is separate from this socially recognized reality. This is a non-social reality, a suspended reality with no premise.

Irving Goffman, who wrote *Frame Analysis*, was one of the few sociologists who fully understood this. He describes the process in which a multi-layered reality is created, as well as the meaning of the fraudulent behavior as part of this process. Goffman refers to the following example.

> A housewife has filed a $100,000 malpractice suit against a psychiatrist. She claimed he prescribed sexual relations with himself as therapy and then charged her for the 'treatments.'
>
> ...In the suit the 33-year-old mother of two said she had held the doctor in 'complete confidence and trust.' He persuaded her, she said, that her problems stemmed from a lack of sexual activity and suggested himself as a sexual partner. She said she agreed to the 'treatments' for several

> months and then became 'worried and remorseful' because he had stopped charging for the visits. Mrs Keene said that when she implored him to stop the treatments, he criticized her sexual abilities and told her he was intimate with her only because she 'was so available.' Then he billed her for $225 (Goffman 1986: 160).

If one were to simplify the intricate groups of concepts used by Goffman[4], this example would represent a 'fabricated' act by a 'conman'. The treatment carried out at the medical location represented a socially recognized format and the con would not be exposed as long as this was adhered to. In this example, the sexual act itself was the treatment and the anti-social act of the sexual act has been buried under the social reality of medical treatment. In the world of 'fabrication' described by Goffman, the issue is not the 'intention' or 'motive' of the person carrying out the con but, as conveyed by the title, it is the 'subject' hidden in the 'place' or the frame that is created by the con. The only matter of importance is how the persons (the conman and his sympathizer/s) carrying out the act appear, as they gamble on superficiality and the frame that is created. The duality of the self such as 'the real self' and 'the performing self' is of no concern[5].

In the way that the example of the housewife and the psychiatrist conveys how reality can consist of both a social element and an anti-social element, people also live in both a social reality and an anti-social reality. For example, when Ōbayashi was working at the Tochigi Branch of the Ashikaga Bank she was in the socially accepted position of a 'bank employee'. At the same time, however, she was in a secret relationship with Abe. The latter represents the socially unrecognized reality. However, it is only the conman that is immune to this duality of realities, and successively creates realities with no social basis. The aim of this book is to examine society with the suspended reality that the conman inhabits – the so-called degree-zero sociality – as the departure point.

2 Degree-zero Sociality

The degree-zero sociality phase

The relationship between a genuine conman and his sympathizer represents a mutual interchange between two people and corresponds to the sociological term 'interaction.' Sociologists tend to simplistically argue that all interactions are social. However, some situations, as represented by the tuned-in relationship between the conman and the person being deceived by the conman, is absent of any sociality. Let us call this degree-zero sociality.

Time and space are not yet controlled in this phase. A genuine conman disturbs time by rejecting his or her past. As illustrated by the example of the Diet Member who, having lied about his academic record, is not only forced to resign but is held criminally accountable, a personal resume or history is an important device to establish one's sociality. However, for a genuine conman such devices are meaningless. In fact, many no doubt see a resume as nothing more than a product of modern society and one would not have to be a conman to not feel obliged to be bound by its contents. As a result of their encounter with Abe, Ōbayashi and Kashimura found themselves living an anti-social 'time' in which the binding conditions of existence – as symbolized by the resume – did not apply. The regular and orderly time that passed in the bank where Ōbayashi worked had no meaning in the world created by Abe and Ōbayashi[1]. Once someone misappropriates money from a bank and assists a fugitive, then that person becomes immersed in degree-zero sociality.

An alternative definition of the degree-zero sociality phase is that which is controlled by uncertainty or indeterminacy. One does not know what is going to happen in this phase and yet becomes actively involved in the uncertain situation. This is clearly conveyed by Kashimura's comment that she didn't care what happened to her and just wanted to make sure Abe could avoid arrest for even one more day so that she could be with him for just that much longer. In the state that Kashimura was in, what happened to herself was no longer the issue. The time in which Kashimura was living was dictated solely by how she could assist Abe to remain on the run. Although Abe and Kashimura were finally arrested, it took much longer than the police anticipated before they were finally arrested. During this time, Abe and Kashimura moved between motels and hot spring inns in order to 'avoid the police for even one more day' and then began living in Kanazawa. Being a fugitive requires that one makes what one believes is the right decision immediately in response to each situation that arises.

Moreover, in this phase, the boundaries for differentiating space have no meaning. The conman appears in various places and there creates a degree-zero society. In this way, the genuine conman unfastens the 'joints' of space and time.

A valuable reference in the examination of the degree-zero sociality phase and how it relates to social organization is the world of *Tosa Genji* [Genji of Tosa] as described by ethnologist Tsuneichi Miyamoto (Miyamoto 1984). Genji was an old man, over 80 years old, who lived in a village in the mountains of Tosa and was once a horse dealer. Reminiscing about his life, the old man makes the following statement.

> A horse dealer makes money by deceiving people and so the term *bakuro-guchi* (horse dealer-speak) was used to describe people who lied. No one would believe them and they were treated as fools. (abbreviated) They'd bring a no-good, useless cow and tell you that it's a good cow. But after about six months a farmer would turn that bad cow into a good cow. So a good farmer is like a god who can change even pebbles into money through his own efforts. People like that would see us as the scum of society (Miyamoto 1984: 139).

In contrast to the way that the old man saw himself – 'I did nothing for 80 years. My life's been spent deceiving people and lying to women' – Genji of Tosa was not necessarily a conman or scam artist. This is because he played a mediating role in exchange. The old man believes that it is the farmer who adds value through labor that is legitimate, while a horse dealer is nothing more than 'scum.' The old man not only (believes that he has) deceived farmers but also believes that he has deceived many women, which must be how he got the name 'Genji in Tosa' (Author's comment: This name originates from 'Hikaru Genji', the main character of *The Tale of Genji* by Murasaki

Shikibu. Genji of Tosa was probably named after the classic Japanese novel depicting Hikaru Genji's numerous affairs with women). The old man continues:

> Any woman will always forgive you as long as you're good to them. In the end I had so many women that I nearly went blind. I was in so much pain for three days and three nights that I couldn't even see. That's the payback for straying from the straight and narrow. I never did one decent thing. Real men never trusted me. For some reason only women did whatever I wanted them to. (abbreviated) Come to think of it, I never did anything to a woman that she wasn't happy with. I always did what she asked, whatever would make her happy (Miyamoto 1984: 156).

This is something that the conman Abe of the Ashikaga Bank embezzlement incident might have said as an elderly man reminiscing about his past. As mentioned earlier, Abe stated during the trial that he had not intimidated Ōbayashi or been violent towards her. Abe or Genji are both people who free women from the social 'spell.' People like Abe and Genji draw women away from a social place and lead them into a vacuum (the degree-zero sociality phase).

The two women that Genji of Tosa said he remembered most were two wives, one the wife of a bureaucrat and the other of a prefectural assembly member, men of what is regarded as high status. Of importance is the fact that these two women were both dependent on their husband's status. In other words, their existence was almost totally dominated by their husbands' social status to the extent that they themselves almost did not exist. This absence of 'self', a state in which one seems almost not to exist, at the same time, suggests that there is a tendency to place oneself in a state of degree-zero sociality. The appearance of a conman – such as Genji of Tosa – simply elicits this.

Genji of Tosa describes the exchange that is generated in a place separate from society as 'affection.'

> There was only one old woman left at the end. I bet you've lied to a woman at some time in your life. I feel so sorry for women. A woman can sense how a man's feeling and be attentive toward him but most men can't be the same way towards a woman. All I can say is, it's important to be attentive towards a woman. You should never forget those emotions (Miyamoto 1984: 157).

Affection is born in the exchange that takes place in the social world and a remote world, in the 'barn' and the Daishidō temple building where Genji of Tosa slept with his women. In Genji of Tosa's eyes, affection is generated in a place outside the mesh of society's rules.

According to Genji, 'The rules of the village apply when you're in the village and you have to follow those rules. The rules of the village are strict and if you openly ignore those rules then you end up being ostracized.' He says that he 'didn't walk into the village and live according to its rules' (Miyamoto 1984: 157). Genji continued to live his unique (selfish) life in a non-social place. He is suggesting that it is people like himself who are truly able to feel emotions.

The reality in which Genji lives is not bound by clear norms. Even when it comes to buying and selling cows, each sale represents a 'one-off gamble.' Even though a certain set of rules may exist, they are not clearly stated, nor are they shared by everyone involved in the exchange. Although Genji believed that he was deceiving the farmers, the farmers themselves would also have had their own agenda.

One did not have to be a stranger like this horse dealer. There were apparently many people in the villages of Japan 'who had once lived a free-wheeling life on the move' and who were called *sekenshi* [the worldly-wise]. Miyamoto points out that 'although the common perception of people living in villages was one of ordinariness, compared to today – in which, in theory, people verbally express themselves but in fact whose personal lives and activities adhere to a pattern – there were many older people living in villages whose behavior was, frankly, extraordinary' (Miyamoto 1984: 214). Unique people, that is, people living in the degree-zero sociality phase were found in villages. The rules of a village therefore do not necessarily reject creativity. In a way, there is an openness in village life that accepts people such as the cunning and worldly-wise and Genji of Tosa. The villagers in fact gave their leftovers to Genji of Tosa and his wife. In the end, Genji makes the following statement:

> After we've had dinner, the old woman goes round to the farmer's houses to collect any leftovers. That's her job and she does it every day come rain or wind. I just sit here like this. I only ever walk down to the riverbed to do my business or go into the water…It's been 30 years since I lost my sight – it seems a long time but also not so long. I still remember all those women. They were all kind, good women (Miyamoto 1984: 158).

Villages are certainly controlled by a strict set of rules. In this sense, a village is closed. However, the village did not attempt to expel the blind man and his wife. If anything, the villagers were looking after the two's welfare by giving them their leftovers.

As we can see from Genji's story, villagers live according to the village's rules (norms). A symbolic violence is exerted against the villagers. At the same time, however, a void exists in the village where rules do not intervene. This is not recognized as social reality. At times, however, it can be gradually recognized socially while in other cases it can simply end as a void. The reason why the villagers gave their leftovers to Genji and his wife is because, in one sense, the existence of this void has been recognized by the village.

It is possible to expediently establish two categories. The first category is the world created by those who, like the ordinary villagers, live according to the rules. This includes not only villages of the past but also contemporary corporate organizations. However, this does not mean that the lives of the villagers or businessmen are totally controlled by rules and that there is no opportunity (void) for the intervention of imagination. People are always living a double reality. The salarymen carry out the work demanded of them but this does not mean that they completely relate to the role allocated to them within the organization[2]. Moreover, the entry of a stranger is not necessarily rejected by the boundaries of the village or the corporate organization. There is always a void.

The other category is the world without any clear boundaries, governed by uncertainty or indeterminateness and not necessarily controlled by norms. This is the world in which the genuine conman dwells. However, this world does not exist parallel to and separate from the other world with boundaries. It is a world that suddenly appears in a void that exists in the world with boundaries, only to disappear again. At times, however, this world can become a center and a space with established boundaries. In many cases this world is criticized for being anti-social by those living in the world of boundaries.

People such as Genji of Tosa appear in a village and then disappear. However, a village or a State can not exist without these people. Life in the village could not exist if there were no horse dealer to resell cows. Despite the fraudulent aspect to the transaction that took place between the horse dealer and the villagers, this was not recognized as such. There is no strict adherence to the concept that an exchange should be equivalent. These two different worlds are closely intertwined to create an integrated world.

In this sense, as Shun Inoue points out, 'Society can not exist in a place where scams can not exist' (Inoue 1999: 91). Society is clearly built on a system of trust but at the same time scams and cons are also an element of society (Inoue 1999: 93). In other words, there are two aspects to society, that of 'trust' and that of 'scams or cons.' However, many of those who theorize on society, including sociologists, have only ever addressed 'the system of trust.' Rather, they have remained unaware that it is behind trust that scams and cons lie. 'A system of scams' is not visible because of the absence of any official rules.

It is unclear as to which act represents fraud and which represents gift-giving in the degree-zero sociality phase. The issue has never been about whether an act is moral or immoral. There is, however, a certain type of order even in such a phase, a place that enables the act to take place and be executed without interruptions. The only issue in this process is tuning into the same wavelength as the other[3].

Fraud as crime

A genuine conman does not try and force the other party over to his side. In other words, power is not an issue with the conman. This means that he has no interest in achieving social status. Normally, as 'an individual', one belongs to a certain position in society and has a desire to realize a higher position. A genuine conman, however, is indifferent to social status and in fact can not relate to it. The conman simply makes others want to give him money.

The conman establishes a particular relationship with the other person whom he or she is attempting to deceive. It is at this point that the conman emits a particular energy. However, this imaginary world that is created between them does not last for long. The fascination of a fraudster eventually disappears just as an odor eventually disappears. Therefore, a genuine conman is constantly standing by so that he can move away, that is, escape. A prerequisite for a conman is that he has the ability to move quickly. He goes on the run, skillfully ensuring that he can never be identified and carries out a new con in his next destination. In the movie *The Sting*, the two conmen played by Paul Newman and Robert Redford set up an imaginary off-site betting shop with the cooperation of their friends and con an enormous amount of money from a major criminal and an enemy of the Redford character. The last scene in the movie is after the victim has been conned, everyone quickly dismantling the off-site betting shop and leaving the site.

The escape route taken by Abe who was involved in the Ashikaga Bank embezzlement incident was quite extensive and it began on July 20, 1975. Abe phoned Ōbayashi at home in order to receive the money and the two were to meet at the parking lot of a bowling center in Tochigi City. As the embezzlement by Ōbayashi was discovered five days earlier, the Tochigi police had six unmarked police cars on standby. Despite this, Abe and his accomplice, who sensed danger, skillfully slipped through the police net and managed to escape. The September 11 edition of *Shūkan Shinchō* magazine quoted one of the policemen involved in the ambush – 'Abe was surrounded and escape would have been impossible under normal circumstances, and yet he managed to escape by crashing his car into each of our patrol cars.'

By this stage Abe had begun living with Kashimura (refer chapter1). Kashimura divorced her husband on 16 July and moved into the apartment in Tokyo that had been rented by Abe. On the 20th, she went shopping to purchase items for the couple's new home and on her return received a call from Abe who instructed her to 'leave the apartment immediately and book into a hotel' (Sawachi 1976). Abe stayed with Kashimura and three of his accomplices in the hotel and then bid farewell to Kashimura, intending to flee the country alone. He got as far as Haneda airport but in the end was unable to make the decision to leave and phoned Kashimura on the 22nd. Kashimura, overjoyed that Abe was still in the country, met up with him again to find out that out that he was wanted by the police. 60 days of life on the run began. The couple traveled through Odawara, Kōfu, Mino Ota, Uozu, Niigata, Akita, Toyama, Maizuru, Tamatsukuri Onsen, Yonago, Tottori, Hamasaka, Kaga Onsen, eventually renting an apartment in Kanazawa. As referred to in chapter 1, the couple lived there for around a month under the guise of a young man sitting his university entrance exams and his sister. However, they left the apartment when they learnt that a police officer was carrying out a residency check in the area. After spending the night at a hotel, Kashimura left Abe waiting in a coffee shop while she went to a bank to withdraw money, where she was arrested. Concerned that Kashimura had not returned, Abe contacted an employee of International Union Development Center, a company that Abe had set up, and was told that Kashimura had been arrested. Abe was arrested on his return to Tokyo.

That it took longer than anticipated before Abe was arrested is conveyed by an article published in a weekly magazine at the time.

According to *Shūkan Shinchō* (August 28 1975 edition), after Abe had managed to escape from the Tochigi carpark, 'over 30 investigators were dispatched to Tokyo, but for some reason the police were having difficulties predicting where Abe might turn up and as a result "it turned into a long-term campaign."' Kashimura's assistance was of great significance in Abe's escape. In her statement, Kashimura said that 'life was hard but I felt totally fulfilled' and that 'I didn't care what happened to me, I just wanted to make sure Abe could avoid arrest even for one more day so that I could be with him for just that much longer' (Sawachi 1976).

The 'pure' relationship between the conman and his sympathizer that existed between Kashimura and Abe remained intact until the end. It is this point that is of interest in the relationship between Abe and the women who became involved with him. In many cases, however, there eventually comes a time when the conman finds himself having to defend himself after being questioned by those who realize that they have been victims of a con or scam. In some cases a conman ends up killing his victim as he can no longer avoid any more questions and fears that the scam will be revealed. By this stage, the world that has been created by the conman and his sympathizer has dissolved. In other words, the conman does not always get away.

It is in this way that a con or scam becomes 'an incident' but this does not necessarily mean that it ends up as a criminal case. It becomes an incident when a third person, who is not involved, realizes that what has taken place is a con or scam. In *Frame Analysis*, Goffman addresses the process in which this 'incident' takes place or the process until it becomes an incident. The same applies to situations in which the conman's sympathizer is unable to fully appreciate the imaginary world created by the conman and, dissatisfied, asks for the conman to pay back the money he has given him. In such a situation, it is the sympathizer who, in a sense, becomes the third person.

There are, however, those who attempt to maintain the imaginary world that they have so skilfully created. This type of conman not only attempts to ensure that his lies aren't exposed but goes as far as to create a false theoretical system. Let us call the conman who loses his genuineness and instead attempts to prescribe meaning to his own actions as the 'moral conman.'

The moral conman can be seen as 'charismatic', as described by Max Weber (Weber 1956). Charisma is attributed to people who are endowed with supernatural or superhuman powers. Whether such powers have an objective basis is not the issue. All that matters is that those who are controlled by or submit to that charisma believe that the charisma exists. It is this charisma and its believers that create the rules. According to Weber, not only historically famous heroes and religious figures, but 'sophisticated charlatans' and 'hack-writers selling groundless stories' can also have charisma. However, there is a difference between charlatans and religious figures. This is because the charlatan has no desire for power. Conmen who, like charlatans, do not desire power are genuine conmen, in contrast to religious figures and heroes who are moral conmen.

The moral conman's strategy

The moral conman uses various strategies to wield influence. Let us first examine the characteristics of these strategies by comparing this type of conman with the genuine conman (Ogino 1976b: 95–9).

The introduction of the concept of time

Even though he may have made a promise for the future such as marriage, a genuine conman has no intention of marrying. Even promises are nothing more than playthings for the conman to enjoy his preposterous or irony-filled imaginary world. The conman instantly transforms himself into a US Air Force pilot or the president of a company and yet makes no attempt at making the sort of effort that would normally be required of a genuine corporate president. He simply claims that he is the president, playing the role for as long as his lie is not exposed. In an imaginary world the conman can instantly be transformed into a president and therefore he becomes the president, not believing for a moment that he should be making an effort into maintaining that position. The only attempt that the genuine conman makes is to be true to the unique world that he has created. No parallel exists anywhere else and nor is there any alternative.

As a result, the genuine conman has absolutely no desire for upward mobility. Similarly, the desire, like Cinderella, to be chosen by a Prince and become his Princess, does not represent a desire to make one's way in the world by, for example, 'ruling the world' like the great samurai Toyotomi Hideyoshi. In other words, as long as one does not ascend the hierarchy, then equally one can not fall. If the lie is exposed then all one has to do is escape to another place and once again transform oneself. In this way, the genuine conman destroys hierarchy in a flash and only for a flash.

However, the moral conman attempts to establish a hierarchy that allows him to be at the top. Unlike the world of the genuine conman, in this world the worship of this hierarchy that will enable the moral conman's desire for upward mobility to be realized has already begun. The desire for upward mobility introduces the concept of time which inevitably has no value in the world of pure imagination. And, to ensure that it does not remain just a concept, it is refined so that it is as real as possible. An ideal world is established and one must actually make an effort towards its realization. This requires training and practice. This therefore means that the transformation in the 'here and now' as directed by the genuine conman is no longer possible. Complete transformation is carried forward to the future.

Establishing norms and boundaries

Having to train and practice equates to the establishment of various norms. This is the definitive difference between the genuine conman and the moral conman. The genuine conman is tolerant and shuns discrimination. The establishing of norms, however, introduces exclusivity into the world of the genuine conman which is characterized by acceptance. The conman becomes selective and differentiates between those who are chosen and those who aren't. It is at this point that morality is established. Those who are chosen personify goodness and those who are not chosen are seen as 'bad.' The freedom and fairness that characterizes the genuine conman are lost and the conman instead aims to apply a justice based on a selective morality. It is a discriminatory and exclusive justice.

The establishment of power through the enforcement of morality requires a place for that morality to come into effect. This is related to the establishment of boundaries. The conman who has become a moralist draws a boundary between those who agree with him and those who do not, and tries to exclude those who do not agree with him. The genuine conman will go anywhere as long as there is the possibility of a coincidental encounter. There are those who, like Abe, wait on the train for their victim, while others will join an organization. As the conman becomes a moralist, however, this mobility is lost and he attempts to settle in one location. The buildings named *satian* that were built by the Aum Shinrikyō cult at the foot of Mt Fuji is a typical example of such a location.

However, in many cases the moral conman's 'enclosure' – which the *satian* was – has the effect of highlighting the conman's ignominiousness. Although this may initially seem paradoxical, the secret world that rejects the presence of a third party is much easier to maintain without any spatial restrictions. In order to protect a secret, it is better that there is no specific location. The genuine conman has no fixed address and moves from one location to another. The moral conman, however, attempts to set up a home. There is a strong possibility, however, that this will result in his secret being exposed. Because he wants to prevent this, the threshold of the boundaries that the moral conman sets is raised too high. The surveillance carried out to protect the secret inside the boundaries becomes more intense.

The most effective strategy to protect the secret that lies inside is not to allow strangers to look in. The moral conman, by accepting anyone who wants to look in, maintains the attitude of acceptance of the genuine conman but must also reject those who do not sympathize with his ideology. While the moral conman gathers together large numbers of sympathizers/victims into the location that he has enclosed, he must also be vigilant and make sure that any spectators who don't sympathize with him do not manage to slip inside. A typical method used to ensure this is solicitation. In the same way that a genuine conman preys on his victim, solicitation is also often carried out on busy streets. There are many ways solicitation is carried out and these include handing out questionnaires, or informing people of an interesting meeting to which they are invited. Regardless of the type of solicitation, however, the true nature of the solicitation is not revealed at the time. The people being solicited are first reassured and then later gradually drawn into the world of the moral conman.

However, even though the solicitation results in gaining sympathizers, there are always those who will try and leave the organization. There is also the possibility that outsiders will try and sneak inside. Physical violence is therefore exerted to maintain the secret that lies inside. A second-rate conman will be violent because he fears that his victim could expose him, but the moral conman will morally justify the violence that is exerted. More appropriately, morality unavoidably demands the exertion of violence. The exclusivity generated by morality, the tendency to eliminate those who do not adhere to morality inevitably generates violence. There is a strong connection between morality or ideology and violence.

From a tuned-in relationship to distancing

In this way, the moral conman distances himself from his sympathizers. This is in contrast to the genuine conman who attempts to close the distance between himself and his sympathizers. The moral conman categorizes others into those who already sympathize with him, those who have the potential to be sympathizers (the targets of solicitation), and those who are hostile to him. The conman establishes his position by clarifying the distance in these different categories.

Uniforms and costumes are used to realize this. As can be seen in the Nazi uniform or the Aum Shinrikyō costume, the moral conman uses external appearances to convey the oneness between himself and his sympathizers.

Meanwhile, however, the genuine conman does not demand that his sympathizer alters his appearance in order to control him. Jonaf Elizabeth Kuhio, mentioned in chapter 1, had cosmetic surgery on his nose, dyed his hair brown and wore a military uniform but this was nothing more than a performance. Kuhio was simply attempting to differentiate himself from others and did not demand that others emulate him. If anything, he rejected emulation.

In contrast, the moral conman makes himself a model for his sympathizers and encourages them to emulate him. Emulating the model's external appearance does not collapse the distance between the conman and the sympathizer, and in actual fact creates distance. This is because emulation can only take place when the object of emulation is worthy of emulation and is the object of reverence or aspiration, or if not, at least is in a significantly higher position than his emulators. Emulation can only take place when there is a distance – between the emulator and the model or object of emulation – that can not be buried. Because of this, subtle differences are extended even to uniforms and costumes (difference in color, for example). There is a difference between the moral conman and his sympathizers. Even sympathizers are differentiated depending on rank. It is through such strategies to create distance that the moral conman extends his influence.

The truth about spectators

The moral conman uses various strategies to establish his legitimacy. It is these very strategies, however, that not only increases the number of sympathizers but also creates enemies. For example, solicitation is a much more obvious act than the genuine conman's advances. The wearing of strange costumes would attract even more attention. It is at this stage that moves are generated to alienate those sympathetic to the moral conman are generated. People criticizing the foolishness of those who continue to blindly give money to the moral conman begin to emerge. People begin to warn others that a questionable cult is soliciting members of the general public.

As in the illiterate society described by Tsuneichi Miyamoto, in a world in which people were relatively uninterested in distinguishing between truth and lies (refer chapter 1), such adversaries rarely made an appearance. As mentioned in chapter 1, however, when the guarantee of certainty in life (or the avoidance of risk) became a dominant view amongst people, people sensitive to the existence of moral conmen began to appear. Let us call these people the spectators.

Most important for the spectators is the guarantee of certainty in life, the understanding that 'labor definitely creates wealth' and 'both parties in an exchange will profit.' The tendency for the spectators to have a hostile view of new organizations is because they feel that the certainty of their positions, their safety zone, is being threatened. That is why spectators feel anxious about anything foreign. The spectators have also always tried to avoid involving themselves in anything new.

In order to guarantee certainty in life, it is necessary to be able to strictly differentiate between what is real and what is false, between truth and lies. Certainty of life based on reality and truth can only be possible when 'lies' and what is 'false' are eliminated and 'truth' and what is 'real' continually examined. The spectator evaluates the position of clarifying the truth, and, as is carried out in the study of history or law, attempts to interpret the imaginary world within the context of moral knowledge that defines such a world as either unreal or a simple fantasy. Reality, historical reality and legal reality are created and, for the first time, fraud is socially recognized as a crime (an awareness of which does not exist in illiterate societies).

However, having said that, this spectator morality is of no use whatsoever to people who are longing to be deceived/saved. An empathetic relationship exists between the conman and the deceived, and the con will not be uncovered as long as the latter has no doubts whatsoever about giving all his possessions to the conman. When this is considered, we can conclude that it is the evaluation of the spectators that influences whether the moral conman can further extend his power. If the moral conman desires success, he must completely exclude, and indeed assimilate, the spectators.

Mito Kōmon as conman

How, then, can the spectators be assimilated? The television drama *Mito Kōmon* illustrates how this is done.

Mito Kōmon is a story about Vice-Shogun Tokugawa Mitsukuni (Mito Kōmon) who, under the guise of a retiree, traveled the land ridding society of evil. Mito Kōmon would remain in disguise and in the end (in reality Kaku-san, Kōmon's attendant) holds up the *inrō* [small box with a crest] to reveal his true identity. At least twice during each episode, Kōmon is transformed from Tokugawa Mitsukuni into a *chirimen* fabric wholesaler and then back to Tokugawa Mitsukuni. In some episodes Kōmon undergoes more than two transformations. One episode features a crooked fortuneteller who profiteers by conning the townspeople. The owner of a long-established inn so blindly believes the fortuneteller that he falls under his control and ends up neglecting the family business. Kōmon and his entourage stay at this inn, where a concerned member of the inn owner's family asks Kōmon for his help. Kōmon competes with the crooked fortuneteller by telling fortunes using an abacus. Kōmon, disguised as a fortuneteller, begins to expose the evil deeds of the fortuneteller, whom Kōmon has already investigated. In this episode, Kōmon undergoes three transformations.

The reason Kōmon so easily transforms himself from *chirimen* fabric trader to fortuneteller is not part of his strategy to punish the evildoers. It is simply because Kōmon has always excelled at transforming himself and is in fact a rare conman far superior to the conmen mentioned so far, such as Abe or Kuhio. For Kōmon, bringing to his knees a charlatan fortuneteller who was nothing more than a second-rate moral conman, was an easy task.

Because he is a moral conman, Kōmon persuades and lectures others. He tells townspeople that families should cooperate and work hard in the family business, while he tells samurai not to abuse power. However, Kōmon does not spend a lot of time lecturing these people, only speaking when required. He behaves as though there is an unspoken understanding amongst everyone that family love and hard work are virtues and so there is no need to lecture on these topics. The morality advocated by Kōmon is absolute and unshakable.

Depending on the situation, Kōmon is prepared to use force against those who act immorally. The evil and immoral, or spectators who doubt his morality, must be brought to justice to ensure that Kōmon's morality is adhered to. Kōmon naturally never personally attempts to exert force against these evil people. He makes sure that the evildoers driven into a corner or the second-rate conman always makes the first move so that the violence that he exerts appears as self-defense. As a result, Kōmon uses violence to force his opponents to surrender and yet the impression given is that he had no choice but to use force. Kōmon behaves as though he has the right to exert violence while conveying that the exertion of force itself should only be the last resort.

In the climactic scene in which the evildoer threatening Kōmon's morality is punished, the viewer comes under the illusion – though temporary – that the entire world is dominated by Kōmon's morality. In this world, no one threatens Kōmon. No one doubts Kōmon's authority, and no one sees Kōmon as a fool brandishing his *inrō* to show off his authority. Anyone who doubts the authority symbolized by the *inrō* is either eliminated violently or lectured.

This means that Kōmon, who never reveals his true identity until the climactic scene, had deceived everyone. And yet no one condemns Kōmon as a conman. The townspeople in the story are happy to learn that they were deceived by Kōmon. Believing in the authority of the *inrō*, they feel grateful, and if anyone were to claim that Kōmon's *inrō* had no power, he would probably be eliminated by the townspeople. This is how much the experience of being complicit in the authority symbolized by Kōmon's *inrō* generates a deep sense of satisfaction.

When the moral conman completely eliminates the spectators to take control of the world, that world closely resembles the secret world created by the genuine conman. In this world, the moral conman is in fact not seen as a conman. The people no longer peer in as spectators on the outside, instead discovering a sense of satisfaction at continuing to be deceived by the conman. They are not only seeking a direct benefit, but also experience a purpose in life knowing that they are co-conspirators with authority. As long as they experience this sense of satisfaction, they never doubt that power itself is fraught with fraud. It is at this stage that the order that the moral conman attempted to create reaches its completion. Order must therefore continue to be supported by the people who actively choose to be deceived.

Mito Kōmon is a story about a successful moral conman. There is a clear reason why this long-running television program has continued to rate so well. The viewers, unlike the characters that appear in the drama, already know that Kōmon is actually a *chirimen* fabric trader. Kōmon's double transformation – from Vice-Shogun to *chirimen* fabric trader and back again – is concealed from the characters in the drama and this secret is only known to the viewers = the spectators. The viewers know, from the beginning of the drama, what the 'conman' Kōmon is plotting and their knowledge of his secret is a source of pleasure for them. For example, even if a charlatan fortuneteller appears in the drama, the viewers already know that Kōmon's powers as a conman are overwhelmingly superior. Because they recognize the secret authority that lies behind Kōmon, they are able to acknowledge and affirm Kōmon's powers.

The characters in the drama who are saved by Kōmon become aware of his double transformation when Kōmon takes out his *inrō*. It is then that they, like the viewers, realize the secret of his power. They become aware that they have been conspiring with authority and are joyous in their realization that this authority has established order in their lives. Kōmon's double transformation, which the characters in the drama immediately realize when the *inrō* is revealed to them, is appreciated by the viewers. In the end, as they watch the climactic scene, the viewers become one with the characters who are saved/deceived by Kōmon. The viewers can relate to the people who were so innocently deceived by authority. *Mito Kōmon* enables us to experience the joy of secretly conspiring with power and the joy of being deceived by power.

This is related to the fact that the characters in the drama share amongst themselves the sense of order which must be strongly felt in the climactic scene. This sense of order represents the amorphous desire of being seduced, which has already been developed in the one-on-one relationship between the professional conman and his victim. The fraudster only reveals his secret (although it is a false secret) to the person he is trying to deceive in order to gain their cooperation. The person being deceived – regardless of whether he is aware of the conman's plot or not – rejoices in the fact that he is sharing this secret with the conman and 'invests' in the conman's plot. The conman is not exposed as long as this 'investment' generates either a tangible or intangible profit or salvation (Ogino 1997b: 105–110).

An example is the novel *Don Quixote* which depicts the process in which everyone pretends to be deceived so that eventually 'reality' is created.

Don Quixote believes that he is a medieval knight. According to Schutz, 'To Don Quixote there really is a fortress with towers in shining silver, a dwarf's trumpet announcing the approaching knight, beauteous maidens taking the air at the castle's gate, and a castellan. Only to the observer there is an inn, a swineherd blowing his horn, two women of easy virtue and an innkeeper' (Schutz 1976: 142). In this way, 'an ordinary metal basin from a barber shop' becomes

'Manbrino's strange basin.' The reason why strangers don't see this as an ordinary basin is because a good witch ensures this and thus protects the basin.

However, in Part 2 of *Don Quixote*, Don Quixote's 'Adventures' are published and everyone who encounters Don Quixote has read this book. The readers begin to behave as though they are in Don Quixote's world. For example, the Duchess goes to the trouble of pretending to be 'deceived' by Don Quixote. However, in contrast, Don Quixote begins to doubt the world that he had himself believed in. In the end, he accepts the ordinary, everyday world.

Viewers of *Mito Kōmon*, like the characters such as the Duchess who appears in *Don Quixote,* experience a sense of superiority through the drama because they are aware of the secret of power. As viewers = spectators, in the end, just like the characters in the story, they forget that they are spectators and find themselves wanting to surrender to Kōmon's moral authority. One of the most effective strategies in dissolving any skepticism by the spectators towards morality is to ensure that they know the secret and tricks of power and yet happily accept being deceived.

Whether a political system is a democracy or a totalitarian state is a secondary issue in comparison to the issue of how to address criticism by spectators. Of importance when creating order is to create a *sense* of order, that is, a sense that the people are colluding with authority. This is what validates authority. If the moral conman is to establish a justified power, he must first consider how to address the suspicious rather than the credulous. There are several 'measures' that can be used, including a conciliatory approach to lure them, or to violently eliminate them using one's supporters. Regardless of the method used, a moral conman who does not know how to deal with spectators cannot survive.

Incidentally, the real Mito Kōmon (Mitsukuni) apparently never traveled through Japan, as depicted in the drama. And yet the Mito Kōmon in the drama is constantly on the move. There is no need for a sovereign ruler, including Mito Kōmon, to conceal his identity and hit the streets. So why create this 'story' of a sovereign ruler concealing his identity and traveling through Japan?

It is because the story is a symbolic depiction of the mechanism that deems governance as legitimate. Fraud is no longer fraud and a conman becomes a sovereign ruler when the situation is one in which rules are absent. Situations threatening this order arise even after order has been established. It is a new situation that can not be controlled by existing rules. The Italian philosopher Giorgio Agamben, quoting Carl Schmitt's theory that 'rules in fact become effective for the first time when exceptions exist' (Schmitt 1922), calls this state 'the state of exception' (Agamben 1995). This is a situation in which rules no longer apply, order according to the law has been extinguished, and yet complete chaos does not reign. It is more a state that lies on the boundary of order and chaos.

Mito Kōmon transforming himself into a *chirimen* fabric trader signifies a situation in which the rule that 'people should completely obey the Vice-Shogun' does not apply. Situations that the sovereign ruler Mito Kōmon does not see as desirable are taking place. One example is the control wielded by the charlatan fortuneteller. Kōmon establishes order in this case by punishing the 'evil-doer' such as the fortuneteller who is behaving freely (behaving just as he wants to, from Kōmon's perspective).

What is important here is that there is no inherent authority in the morality preached by Kōmon, and it is only by using force to make those who Kōmon defines as 'the enemy' surrender that this morality takes on value. In other words, morals and rules such as laws in themselves do not have an inherent and universal characteristic. They are only created when a situation arises that presents a new threat to order. Because states of exception take place in various locations, Kōmon must continue his travels to confront these 'states of exception.' Although paradoxical, this also indicates that the sovereign ruler himself requires states of exception. It is through states of exception that the sovereign ruler can newly establish rules. That is why Kōmon disguises himself as a *chirimen* fabric trader. Kōmon must first conceal his identity in order to enter a state of exception. Furthermore, Kōmon must also 'exceptionally' exert violence in order to eliminate the forces which threaten authority and which have created the state of exception.

3 Society's Violence

Violence and order

The circumstances in which the moral conman appears differs from the degree-zero sociality phase. The moral conman is attempting to get society to accept his existence and also to separate himself from a state of degree-zero sociality. Because of this, he does not resign himself to exerting violence against those who are antagonistic to him. Let us describe this as a phase in which society normally exists and yet a situation arises that enables the moral conman to exist or to appear, and as a result sociality is at a standstill. Giorgio Agamben's 'exceptional situation' examined in chapter 2 also describes the phase of sociality at a standstill, that is, a shut-down of sociality.

In addition to these two phases – degree-zero sociality and the shut-down of sociality – is another phase in which the successful, Mito Kōmon-like moral conman can be found. When society's powers, bestowed in Mito Kōmon's *inrō*, are being exercised, this is what is generally perceived as social order. Let us call the phase in which physical violence or symbolic violence is systematically exerted, under an already established government, as society's violence phase.

Not only Agamben, but all Western social theorists have focused on the phases of the standstill of sociality and of society's violence. The primary preoccupation has been how best to theorize these two phases. The representative theory is that of 17th Century philosopher Thomas Hobbes. According to Hobbes, there is no notable difference amongst people in terms of intellectual ability or physical strength and, in this sense, all people are equal. However, because people are equal in terms of ability, if multiple numbers of people desire the same thing, the result is conflict, or 'a state of war' in an attempt to bring the other to submission. Therefore, in the natural state (in a world without a ruler), there is a possibility for conflict between individuals which makes it impossible for industry to be established, for wealth to be accumulated, and for the foundations for a prosperous life to be laid. In such a state, life is 'solitary, poor, nasty, brutish and short' (Hobbes 1985: 186).

In order to overcome the state in which one must constantly confront death, people have abandoned the enjoyment of complete freedom, and instead consign to a government the authority to exert power and control. This is because people choose a comfortable life through industry over having to exercise control over others while fearing death. According to Hobbes, in a natural state people are unable to establish a cooperative relationship as they are always confronting each other, and that cooperation is only possible within the structure of a republic. He also points out that an internal breakdown in agreement over what constitutes a republic will result, once again, in a state of war.

Two aspects of Hobbes' theory greatly influenced social science. First was Hobbes' attempt to define the establishment of social order before the establishment of society. The other was Hobbes' proposition that violence is the trigger in establishing order (although Hobbes' theory is not that order is established through the trigger of violence, but rather that order is established as a result of overcoming a state of violence). These two points came to represent the central tenet of social theory in Europe and the United States.

However, the difference between the two phases has often been ambiguous. There has often been confusion between the violence within a community that has already been established, or the violence against external forces (in other words war), and the violence that is (seen as) the drive for establishing order. Therefore there is a need to consider how these two phases have been defined in European and American social theory, and why there has been confusion between the two. To gain a clear picture of reality, it is essential that the phase of degree-zero sociality – examined in the previous chapter – be considered, as well as how the three phases are related.

Agitation and crowds

The first sociologist to seriously consider and propose that violence is the trigger in establishing order was Emile Durkheim.

According to Durkheim, an act is not the result of a rational decision in which the individual considers the consequences of that act, but is the result of a special 'force' (Durkheim 1976). This force is experienced not as pressure but as something that surfaces from deep within oneself. This appears to be similar to Weber's concept of charismatic control as it appeals to irrationality, but there is a significant difference between the two concepts. Weber believes that the decision-making mechanism, which occurs in a separate faculty to that of rational decision-making, is generated between the charismastic force and its believers. In contrast, Durkheim's premise is that there is an invisible force that transcends both charisma and its believers. This, for Durkheim, is social force.

Social force that controls the choice of actions is most effective in situations such as a revolution, in which normal standards are no longer effective. People are transformed in order to exert violence and carry out barbaric acts. This phenomenon is not restricted to revolutions and can also be seen in rituals – typically those carried out by indigenous Australians – in which the participators lose all sense of self and are sent into frenzy. Durkheim describes this state in which members of a community lose all sense of self as a 'state of agitation.'

> One can readily conceive how, when arrived at this state of exaltation, a man does not recognize himself any longer. Feeling himself dominated and carried away by some sort of an external power which makes him think and act differently than in normal times, he naturally has the impression of being himself no longer. It seems to him that he has become a new being....And as at the same time all his companions feel themselves transformed in the same way and express this sentiment by their cries, their gestures and their general attitude, everything is just as though he really were transported into a special world, entirely different from the one where he ordinarily lives, and into an environment filled with exceptionally intense forces that take hold of him and metamorphose him (Durkheim 1976: 218).

Although Durkheim argues that religious notion is borne from the sort of agitation that is seen in rituals and revolutions (Durkheim 1976), he is not explaining, in principle, the connection between the frenzied state related to rituals and the emergence of religious notion. Durkheim instead simply mentions the offering ceremony as corroborative evidence that may be able to support his theory that morality emerges from violence. Before theorizing on the offering ceremony, Durkheim first touches on the role of blood in rituals in which one's own blood is sacrificed in a sacred place to indicate the relationship between bloodletting and religion. He then goes on to theorize that the offering ceremony is the most important aspect of religion. However, Durkheim again has not explained the causal relationship between blood letting, violence and the birth of religion. He assumes the existence of a social force, the whereabouts of which remains unclear, arguing that this social force is necessary for people to live fulfilled lives as part of society. Durkheim also argues that this social force can either create a free and indulgent state or it can become a source of morality and even a force to protect its citizens.

In this sense, Durkheim simply assumes a non-social state in which standards such as revolution and ceremony are ineffective, and without any rigorous verification, repeats the argument that it is from this state that order is established. This is where the ambiguity of the concept of the 'state of agitation' stems from. It was Elias Canetti who reexamined Durkheim's state of agitation as the crowd phenomenon (Canetti 1978).

According to Canetti, individuals lose their names in a crowd. If anything, no one calls another by his or her name. There is no need to know the name of the person who happened to be standing beside you. In a crowd, the barrier lying between individuals is removed and everyone becomes equal. To Canetti, there are two modes of existence – to live socially as an individual or to be liberated from this by becoming a part of the crowd. Moreover, the crowd has violent tendencies, almost as if violence had to be exerted in order to escape the shackles of society. The agitated crowd 'plots murder.' And, 'the crowd has an incomparable degree of conviction and moves to realize this aim' (Canetti 1978: 49).

Canetti believes that the sense of the removal of social shackles is generated in the crowd and it is from here that power originates. This argument eradicates the ambiguity of Durkheim's concept of agitation. Durkheim discusses the passion and blood-letting experienced during a revolution and the agitation generated by religious ceremony from the same perspective. Certainly, both are phenomenologically similar in the sense that people become passionate and violent. However, in contrast to the fact that revolution is a movement that completely rejects the past, a religious ceremony is an act that reaffirms the bonds with one's ancestors – there is a significant difference between the two. Durkheim confuses the crowd that is unrestrained by social rules (as during a revolution) with the community that is already controlled by rules.

Moreover, this confusion also lies in the ambiguity of the French word 'le social.' The literal translation of 'le social' is 'social' but the word actually has two meanings. The first meaning of 'le social' is something that is socially significant, that corrects social wrongs such as inequality, and is specifically used within the context of social policy or enterprise in general. Meanwhile, 'le social' can also mean 'a social issue.' Murder and fraud feature in the 'social interest pages' in Japan and in France. In this context, 'le social' is used as a word that indicates the disreputable or the darker side of humans. The word 'le social' conveys the raw reality of people that can deviate from the norm and found outside a system (Ogino 2001). The agitation of the crowd during a festival is something that takes place within the system and has a socially acceptable and positive meaning. In contrast, revolution is an act that attempts to overthrow society itself and is clearly problematic from the perspective of those who continue to maintain the system. Durkheim's confusion is not unrelated to the ambiguity of the word 'le social.'

Canetti focused on the negative aspect of the word 'le social', and as his departure point, examined people who are not defined by social status. His premise was not the existence of a closed community with clear boundaries. Canetti instead attempted to examine people from the perspective of multiple and coincidental encounters. This point differs from Durkheim whose premise was the existence of the community.

However, Canetti, too, became fixated on his theory that community action and violence are directly related, arguing that the crowd – which represents the cumulative effect of innumerable encounters – has a propensity towards violence. This is because he confused the two phases – that of the standstill of sociality, and that of society's violence.

Violence and social theory

The confusion between the two phases of the standstill of sociality and society's violence is already evident in Hobbes' philosophy. It is manifested in Hobbes' attempt to use the example of the indigenous Americans to demonstrate the existence of the natural condition.

> It may peradventure be thought, there was never such a time, nor condition of warre as this; and I believe it was never generally so, over all the world' but there are many places, where they live so now. For the savage people in many places of *America*, except the government of small Families, the concord whereof dependeth on natural lust, have no government at all; and live at this day in that brutish manner (Hobbes 1985: 187).

Hobbes conveys an image of indigenous Americans by referring to journals written by missionaries and others who traveled to the

American continent. Before Hobbes, Montaigne and La Boetie also theorized that indigenous Indians spent half their lives in battle, and the definition of war as a feature of uncivilized society was common in Western Europe during the 17th Century and continued into the 19th Century. Based on this view of uncivilized society, it became generally accepted that a 'conflict situation' predated the creation of social order. A pattern of uncivilized society = barbaric society = conflict situation was established, resulting in statements such as that by George Simmel.

> As long as inter-territorial commerce remains undeveloped, individual travel is something unknown, and intellectual communities do not transcend the boundaries of the group, war is the only sociological relation between different peoples (Simmel 1955: 33).

According to Simmel, war was the catalyst for 'exchange' between communities. The theory that wars were carried out regularly amongst uncivilized societies to improve solidarity continued to be accepted. For example, cooperation between 'us' is guaranteed in uncivilized societies by clarifying the difference between one's enemies and one's allies through war. According to Pierre Clastres, this is how war became normalized (Clastres 1997). There are obviously other theories to explain war. For example, Maurice Davie seeks an economic explanation for war amongst uncivilized societies. As uncivilized societies struggle with poverty they have no choice but to carry out acts of plunder in order to survive, and this is what results in war between tribes (Davie 1931). Meanwhile, Lévi-Straiss stated that 'law is the consequence of the unfortunate result of unsuccessful transaction' (Lévi-Strauss 1943). Clastres criticized Lévi-Strauss' view, saying that it represents nothing other than economism which is little different to Davie's statement that 'commerce is often an alternate solution to war' (Davie 1931: 302), pointing out that this theory has been rejected by economic anthropologists in recent years.

However, uncivilized society and a natural state do not represent the same thing. Uncivilised society is literally already a 'society.' The violence that is being exerted in this society is society's violence and differs from violence in a natural state in which sociality has come to a standstill. Despite this difference, debate on this subject continues today without a clear distinction, between the two phases.

This can also be seen in Rene Girard's popular debate related to offering ceremonies. According to this theory, offering ceremonies repeat the violence that is exerted during the process of the establishment of social order. According to Girard, the ritual of live sacrifices represents the vestiges of primordial violence that was exerted in order to establish order. It argues that primordial violence specifically represents a lynching against a specific person, and that even mythologies linked to offering ceremonies are a symbolic depiction of lynching (Girard 1987). In this sense, mythologies are a fraudulent device to conceal primordial violence.

An example is the following indigenous American Ojibwe myth.

> The five 'original' clans are descended from six anthropomorphic supernatural beings who emerged from the ocean to mingle with human beings. One of them had his eyes covered and dared not look at the Indians, though he showed the greatest anxiety to do so. At last he could no longer restrain his curiosity, and on one occasion he partially lifted his veil, and his eye fell on the form of a human being, who instantly fell dead 'as if struck by one of the thunderers.' Though the intentions of this dread being were friendly to men, yet the glance of his eye was too strong, and it inflicted certain death. His fellows therefore caused him to return to the bosom of the great water. The five others remained among the Indians, and 'became a blessing to them.' From them originate the five great clans or totems (Girard 1987: 105–6).

Lévi-Strauss had theorized on this myth before Girard (Lévi-Strauss 1985), and interprets it as a process in which 'discontinuity' (culture) is introduced and order established (Lévi-Strauss 1964) by 'eliminating' a member of society from that society.

Girard's argument is an extension of Lévi-Strauss' theory. However, in contrast to the fact that Lévi -Strauss sees the depiction of mythology as a symbolic one, Girard, on the other hand, attempts to interpret the murder that was actually carried out in the myth. According to Girard, this is conveyed by the description of the supernatural being who, after killing the human, is sent back to the bottom of the ocean. What matters to Girard is the live burial of the supernatural being, and the prior death of the character is only of secondary importance. However, what can be read into the Ojibwe myth that Girard analyzes is that the male character died as the result of the 'power of the gaze' of a supernatural being. Secondly, as a result, the supernatural being had no choice but to return to the bottom of the ocean. What is clear from then is that because the supernatural being led the male to his death, this resulted in a confrontation between the supernatural being and the Indians but that this confrontation was settled by eliminating the supernatural being that caused the conflict. Certainly, mythology is a symbolic expression and various interpretations are possible. However, in the case of the Ojibwe myth, the argument that the supernatural being is a symbolic expression of lynching by 'someone' is nothing more than conjecture.

According to Girard, the violence of primordial society is not only concealed in the Ojibwe myth but in many other myths. When considering Girard's argument, one does not have to think very hard before realizing that the speculation that lynching establishes social order is anomalous. If a member of an organization committed murder every time the organization faced a crisis, then eventually only one person would remain. When examining this from a historical perspective, too, lynching only ever takes place when organizations are in its last throes. From the Japanese Red Army's lynching incident through to bullying, violence within an organization can never overcome a crisis.[1]

Certainly, the 'sacrifice' of a member of society is tacitly accepted in many societies. Even though we know that deaths from motor vehicle accidents will never be totally eliminated, no law will ever prohibit the manufacture and sales of motor vehicles. However, if the number of victims becomes excessive and the number of victims continues to grow, then motor vehicles would become a device for producing deaths and therefore the number of victims would have to be maintained below a certain level. Although I will not elaborate here, a simple argument such as Girard's is not able to rigorously analyze the relationship between violence and social order.

However, this accessibility of Girard's analysis conveys the characteristics and the limitations of Western social theory since Hobbes. These can be summarized into the following three points.

1. The trigger for the establishment of order lies in the exertion of violence.
2. There is a tendency to seek the grounds for this violence in uncivilized society.
3. (It is revealed that) the exertion of violence, the trigger for the establishment of order, is concealed.

The theory that examines 'violence that is exerted when order is established' within the context of uncivilized society is specific to European and American social theory. And yet European and American societies were established through the exertion of violence. As typically depicted by the French Revolution, the modern state was created by the slaying of enemy forces. Few people criticize the French Revolution today and it is viewed positively, because it is seen as creating a society based on the ideals of freedom and equality. There is rarely any mention of the fact that the French Revolution produced a huge death toll estimated at two million. The fact that the creation of the modern state required violence to be exerted has been concealed, and instead this use of violence has been projected onto 'uncivilized' society, even though we do not know whether violence was as necessary to uncivilized society as it has been to the modern state.

Society's fraud

From the establishment of order through exerting violence to the concealment of that violence: this is the basic schema that has been presented by Western social theory. This schema is clearly evident in the writings of 17th Century French philosopher Blaise Pascal.

Pascal believed that, in the same way that a man walking alone gives way to another who is accompanied by four attendants, power first and foremost represents strength in numbers and that power is established by the majority (Pascal 1995). Although he did not cite uncivilized peoples, according to Pascal power underpins the legitimacy of control. While the forces of various 'classes' remain antagonistic towards each other, conflict surrounding power remains and this force is openly bared, with one class eventually bringing another under its control and rule. From this point, the ruling class does not simply exert force but begins to appeal to people's 'imaginations.' Pascal makes the following statement.

> Our magistrates have shown themselves well aware of this mystery. Their red robes, the ermine in which they swaddle themselves like furry cats, the law-courts where they sit in judgment, the fleurs de lys, all this august panoply was very necessary. If physicians did not have long gowns and mules, if learned doctors did not wear square caps and robes four times too large, they would never have deceived the world, which finds such an authentic display irresistible. If they possessed true justice, and if physicians possessed the true art of healing, they would not need square caps; the majesty of such sciences would command respect in itself. But, as they only possess imaginary science, they nave to resort to these vain devices in order to strike the imagination, which is their real concern, and this, in fact, is how they win respect (Pascal 1995: 10–1).

For Pascal, imagination was not just a fantasy or daydream but something material. Specific items such as a fur cape, a courtroom where judgment is handed down, a fleur de lys, mules or long boots or a square cap stimulate the imagination. These are all items for creating an appearance and in this sense the powers of imagination are effectively exerted through the physical body.

Pascal believed that humans, while having the capacity to make rational decisions, were also 'automatons' who either acted unconsciously or in accordance with their emotions, and furthermore that reason was sluggish and soon found itself 'falling asleep or being confused.' For true worship to be realized, it is not only necessary to persuade the mind with the powers of reason but also to persuade the body that acts unconsciously.

The reason why judges and doctors dress so ostentatiously in order to imbue their knowledge with authority is because they are using their body as a tool of persuasion. This is because it is not logic but the creation of an appearance that is needed to fool others. Although judges and doctors are not conmen, the 'modus operandus' of creating the appearance of possessing, and acting as though they possess certain skills and abilities that they may not have is similar to that employed by the conman. Descartes and Pascal's philosophy represents two different perspectives. The aim behind Cartesian philosophy is to apply reason to negate the very existence of fraud. In contrast, Pascal argues the superiority of the imagination.

Power does not have any validity or basis. The validity of power has simply been established through violence. In order to conceal its lack of validity, an appeal is made to the imagination and a device established to maintain power. Pascal, however, was not completely critical of society's fraud. He was simply depicting this with irony. A certain collusive relationship has been established that only the parties involved are aware of, even in apparently socially recognized relationships (social relationships). A doctor does not simply carry out an examination of a patient and prescribe medication. A good doctor knows how to behave in a way that fulfils the image that the patient has of a doctor. Equally, the patient does not only expect the doctor to make an accurate diagnosis but also anticipates that the doctor will behave as the patient imagines a doctor should. It is a detached perspective in which Pascal believes that a fraudulent element can never be completely eliminated from human relationships.

However, the fraudulent aspect of power in society so ironically depicted by Pascal was criticized by followers of the Enlightenment movement of the 17th Century. Religious believers were labeled *impostures* [impostor]. According to the French dictionary (Le Robert micro 1998), the term *imposture* within this context means 'the abuse of another's goodwill through lying, etc.' It does not simply mean defrauding others of money but encompasses various acts that abuse the goodwill of others. An example is *The Three Impostors – Moses, Jesus and Mohammed* attributed to Baron d'Holbach (Attribué au Baron d'Holbach 1991). This work by a 19th Century Enlightenmentist argues that religion is nothing more than a sham. According to d'Holbach, Moses and the two other founders of religions are nothing more than conmen. Incidentally, the term *escroquerie* describes those who fraudulently obtain small amounts of cash.

Needless to say, this critical theory peaked with the philosophy of Karl Marx, who, during the 19th Century, criticized the fraudulent nature of capitalist society itself. Marx claimed that human history represented a (primarily class) struggle and that the 'communal interests' of one class created an 'imagination.' Because certain classes use 'religion' or 'politics' to control, over time this appears to be something real. Eventually, what has originally only been a product of the imagination become 'the sole determining, active force regulating and active force' (Marx 1991: 60). Marx's argument itself is the same as Pascal's in the sense that Marx argues that religion or philosophy, that represent nothing more than products of the imagination, is used to maintain power that has been obtained through (violent) struggle and that, once the control is complete, that this religion becomes real so that no one then claims that the religion is a product of the imagination.

This argument remained valid amongst 20th Century sociologists. French sociologist Pierre Bourdieu believes that the role of the education system is to transmit knowledge and to carry out a valid assessment of individual ability, and argues that the selection process through examinations, etc simply perpetuates the class structure. For example, telling a labourer's child 'You are a labourer's child', or 'You are vulgar' has an adverse effect on the education system. In fact, this has the potential to create a feeling of rebellion against the education system. However, the use of phrases such as 'this is correct but nothing more', 'nonsense' or 'a monotonous writing style' makes it possible to legitimately eliminate the children of labourers who demonstrate an inferior ability to use the language assessed in schools. Nor is the teacher aware that the method of grading has the effect of eliminating the children of labourers and that he or she is in fact contributing to the perpetuation of the class structure by selecting the children of the ruling class.

> They only do well what they have to do (objectively) because they think they are doing something other than what they are doing, because they are doing something other than what they think they are doing, and because they believe in what they think they are doing (Bourdieu 1996: 39).

'What they have to do (objectively)' refers to the selection of students in accordance with the class that they belong to. However, this can only be carried out consciously by the teacher. The teacher must believe that it is his/her role to evaluate the student in accordance with the student's ability and that this role is being closely carried out. Through this, the teacher exerts 'symbolic violence' against the children of labourers. Bourdieu criticizes the education system that legitimately creates inequality by exerting symbolic violence that perpetuates the existing social structure.

Kyoko Inagaki is more straightforward in arguing that it is the conman who 'exposes the deceptive nature of the education system' (Inagaki 1995: 77). Inagaki analyzes examples such as the conman who repeatedly ate and drank at restaurants only to leave without paying the bill, and cases of fraud involving trading in academic degrees, emphasizing that the actions of conmen who misrepresent their academic history represents nothing more than the lack of validity of the education system itself, and that that the system is simply repaired and consolidated each time the validity of the system is shaken. There is, however, a difference between Bourdieu and Inagaki's perspectives surrounding this issue. Bourdieu's theory simply criticizes the fraudulent nature of the education system. Inagaki, meanwhile, is aware of the duality of reality – that there is a part of the system that is not wholly absorbed by it. In the example of academic fraud raised by Inagaki, a conman called Konakamura claimed to be a student of Teikoku University and asked the residents of a village to help prepare for a large sports festival that was being held by the University. The villagers believed Konakamura and prepared meals for 2,000 people and even flew banners. Because this incident took place in 1892, there was a naivety amongst the villagers – as pointed out by Tsuneichi Miyamoto[2] – that allowed them to believe what they were told. An entire village had easily become immersed in the degree-zero sociality phase.

Anti-critical theory

According to the classification described earlier, critical theory before Bourdieu was suited to the phase of society's violence and was essentially the only phase that was considered. An overwhelming force is involved in the establishment of a community and this same force also strongly binds that community. Moreover, once a community is established, any traces of the violence that was exerted are eliminated, and the reality that any external binding force was exerted is skillfully concealed. However, this does not appear as intrigue, scheming or fraud to those who are being bound. People then turn to the sociologist for an explanation of how exactly this concealment is carried out and how the con is played out.

The sociologists' role is not restricted, however, to merely providing an explanation. The problem with critical theory is that not only does the sociologist take a transcendental perspective but that the sociologist does not question that perspective. Bourdieu, for example, uses the expression 'the role that should be played objectively' but it is sociologists such as Bourdieu who decide what is 'objective.' Consequently, the sociologist is playing God to assess, from this transcendental perspective, what objectivity is. No opportunity is provided to determine whether Bourdieu's decision is indeed correct.

Social science was influenced by system theory that attempted to dismiss this transcendental perspective. Of particular importance is the concept of autopoiesis, introduced by biologists Humberto Maturana and Francisco Varela. According to Hideo Kawamoto, 'The autopoietic system produces the phenomenon of the system through its own activity' (Kawamoto 1991: 271). In other words, the autopoietic system is not affected by external stimulus or environment. To give a simple example, 'as long as autopoiesis is maintained, even with life-systems such as an insect metamorphosizing from a larva to a chrysalis to an adult, the system is perfect at every stage – with the same organic mechanism maintained, the difference only lying in the spatial realization pattern (structure). Only the observer interprets this process as growth. In fact, there is no such thing as growth or progress in an autopoietic system.' According to autopoietic theory, the interpretation of the metamorphosis of insects as 'growth' is nothing more than a reflection of modern values. In contrast, in system theory, the viewpoint of the external observer is removed and 'the actions of the system are depicted from an internal perspective' (Kawamoto 1991: 285).

It was Niklas Luhmann who applied system theory to social science. Communication represents an autopoietic system, autonomously creating itself as a system. When this takes place, communication is realized in the situation described by Luhmann as 'double contingency.' This is a concept that attempts to demonstrate that it is the very inability of two parties which are communicating to completely understand the other's intention (that both parties do not understand is the confusing 'double contingency' that is a condition for communication. Luhmann sees this as an interaction between two black boxes: 'However many efforts they exert and however much time they spend (they themselves are always faster!), the black boxes remain opaque to one another' (Luhmann 1995: 109).

Communication commences despite the fact that, or because, both boxes are black. According to Luhmann, 'The system emerges *etsi no daretur Deus* [even if God doesn't exist]' (Luhmann 1995: 105).

Despite the fact that there is nothing that the two can share in terms of value, the two black boxes establish an 'emergent order.'

As long as a systematic order is generated without any grounds for its existence, 'even if God does not provide anything', then, as argued by Yasuo Baba, systems in general – such as communication systems – are nothing more than 'an empty ring' that can not claim any grounds for its existence. For example, even though the legal system may attempt to claim its validity, in effect 'the law is what the legal system itself views as law' (Baba 2001: 120–2).

A social system in which communication is the smallest unit is essentially indeterminate in nature and is no different from the 'conman' mentioned in this book. Let us recall the relationship between the conman Abe and Ōbayashi as described in chapter 1. The relationship was formed for no reason and was a relationship in which neither ever really knew who the other was. Ōbayashi did not even know Abe's real name until she was arrested. If communication is an emergent order created between two black boxes, the possibilities created by a scam or fraud are always present in communication. In fact, a scam or fraud arguably represents communication at its most fundamental level. From the perspective that a range of different systems, including the legal system, have no real basis or validity as systems and are indeterminate, should make them all fraudulent. From a system theory perspective, however, this is not a derogatory statement. Systems are seen as being inevitably fraudulent. It is this point that represents a major issue in Luhmann's systems theory.

Certainly, the degree-zero sociality phase – the classification referred to in this book – lies at the basis of Luhmann's theory. The tuned-in relationship that is formed between the conman and the victim is maintained by a theory that can not be understood by outsiders, in exactly the same way that a system creates itself. This does not necessarily mean that order is being constantly and emergently established by our increasingly complex society. This is because there is the possibility of a fissure being created in the tuned-in relationship simply by the intervention of a third party. Moreover, there is the possibility of violence being exerted (standstill of sociality).

Luhmann has skillfully avoided the issue of violence by not addressing violence per se and by only examining the process of ongoing confrontation – not the exertion of physical violence – in communication.

According to Luhmann, 'only by repressing such possibilities (= possibilities of allowing physical violence) (i.e., centering them in the political system) can there be adequate freedom for conflict behavior' (Luhmann 1995: 395) and 'as when one party in the conflict kills the other, who then cannot continue the social system of conflict' (Luhmann 1995: 394). Conflict is communication and creates 'a social system.' In contrast, the exertion of violence ('knocking down') 'concludes' conflict and at the same time the social system is extinguished. In other words, from Luhmann's perspective, even if violence was manifested, this represents nothing more than an event 'prior to' the establishment of a social system, and is not a subject of sociological examination nor does it represent an important premise for theorizing society.

The third theoretical perspective

Critical theory exposing the fraudulent nature of the social system itself places too much meaning on the exertion of violence as a trigger for establishing social order, and ignores the degree-zero sociality phase referred to in this book. In contrast to critical theories such as these, it is social autonomy that is the focus of Luhmann's systems theory as well as social theories predating Luhmann's theory such as that of economist Friedrich August von Hayek based on the concept of 'self-organization' (Hayek 1973). A social system is autonomously creating itself and can not be externally adjusted. According to Hayek, justice is something that is created with restraint by society, and he even goes as far as to state that the control and management of society based on a specific program represents a harmful act that goes against the characteristics of a social system.

The idea that individual societies function in accordance with its own theories not only recognizes fraud but also rejects it. I have already pointed out that a relationship that can not be understood by outsiders is formed between the conman and his sympathizer. Amongst the sympathizers of conmen are those who do not accept that he or she has been deceived, even though the conman has been arrested. The deceived continues to believe the conman, even visiting him in prison with gifts. This does not only refer to relationships between two individuals but also to more complex relationships such as organizations that are formed by sympathizers who have submitted themselves to a leader who, in the eyes of outsiders, is nothing more than a conman. Each organization is clearly based on its own theory.

However, if this is completely affirmed, based on the reasoning that society has a self-controlling characteristic, the result is the acceptance of the possibility that decision making by society can be arbitrary. Society is recognized as fraudulent and there is nothing more that can be said. This represents a cavalier view that violence is always erupting in society and that there is always a possibility of cracks appearing. This is the danger of viewing society as an autopoietic system.

Society should not be viewed critically from the observer's position nor should it be viewed intrinsically, denying the fraudulent nature of society. There is a need to explore a third theoretical perspective that represents neither of these. An alternative is provided by the perspective of degree-zero sociality – the pure conman's perspective.

The sociologist must adopt the degree-zero sociality perspective. Reality always contains an aspect of degree-zero sociality. However, social theorists in the United States and Europe are not able to adopt this perspective. This is because theory construction is based on a segmentalization of the world. Critical theorists aim for objectivity by standing outside society, their premise the differentiation between the internal and the external. In systems theory, the premise of which is self-organization, social systems are autonomously produced and it is impossible to objectively view this externally. However, even here, in the sense that the internal and the external of a system are seen as different and what lies within the system can not be known from the outside, with the premise being the differentiation between the inner and outer system, the recognition is similar to that of critical theory. There is a strict differentiation between the internal and the external in both theories, with the premise being that the basis of recognition must be in one or the other of these.

To explain it in more simple terms, only the either–or theory exists in American and European social theory – the answer can only ever be 'yes' or 'no'. Regardless of whether this is rooted in the cultural traditions of Europe and the United States, it is clear that this is related to the proposition that violence is the trigger for establishing order. Violence erupts from a confrontation between two forces and naturally this represents the either–or theory. The two forces confronting each other maintain their ground, demanding a response that is either 'yes' or 'no'. Lévi-Strauss, in *La Pensée Sauvage* points out that 'the principle of theory is that various elements can always be contrasted' and believed that it was 'contrast' or 'confrontation' that represents the very basis of the savage mind (Lévi-Strauss 1962). However, there should be a theory that differs from 'the theory of confrontation' and that could be both 'yes' and 'no' or is neither 'yes' nor 'no'. The either–or theory does not function in the degree-zero sociality phase. In this phase, whether the answer is 'yes' or 'no' is not an issue. There is a need for sociologists to examine reality from the perspective of the degree-zero sociality phase.

4 The Natural State or Sociality at a Standstill

Ethnology and folklore

Folklore knowledge is useful in examining the degree-zero sociality phase and has already been considered in reference to Tsuneichi Miyamoto in chapter 2.

Folklore differs from ethnology or anthropology. As pointed out in chapter 3, in social theory since Hobbes, violence has been viewed as the trigger for the establishment of order, with a tendency to seek the premise for violence in an uncivilized society. In other words, there is a tendency to establish a theory through the representation of 'others.' Ethnology is a study of these 'others' who represent a different culture, and the difference between cultures is the premise and departure point of ethnology. Although this premise began to crumble around the time that Lévi-Strauss devised his structural theory, the examination of relationships with others within the context of the logic of confrontation has remained fundamentally unchanged.

In contrast, the folklore as proposed by Kunio Yanagida is not based on an examination of others but an examination of a more familiar domain. Yanagida claims that 'the observation of one's own environment' (Yanagida 1990: 321) represents the departure point of folklore and that any study 'should begin with one's own community that one understands completely, that is to say "my village."' This theory is not based on the logic of confrontation but on the logic of affinity and is very similar to the tuned-in relationships found in degree zero sociality.[1] A folklore study is only enabled when the logic of affinity exists. Tsuneichi Miyamoto represents this affinity-based study of folklore in practice.

According to Miyamoto 'people in illiterate society were almost ridiculously carefree and honest' (Miyamoto 1984: 252). It was, however, due to this very 'carefree' state that people from such societies were easily deceived. Alternatively, they lived in a society in which the concept of deceiving or of being deceived simply did not exist. When carrying out a sociological examination of this degree-zero sociality phase, both an awareness of and method for examining folklore is necessary.

A village can be confronted by unpredictable events, such as a disaster that injures or even kills residents, or the exertion of violence by others. People always have to deal with such unpredictable situations. Rules are then created to manage these unpredictable situations, and unnecessary conflict can be avoided and the villagers' safety ensured through these rules. In this sense, it is uncertainty that creates rules (Agamben 1995). In the world depicted by Miyamoto, this is represented by 'the laws of the village.'

Meanwhile the uncertainty that the world always faces can at times represent something positive. *Bakuro* [horse dealer] and *sekenshi* [the worldly-wise] such as Genji of Tosa, about whom Miyamoto writes, survive in a state of degree-zero sociality but at the same time function as mediators who provide a link between other villages. Uncertainty does not always represent the negative aspect of an uncertain future; it does not necessarily trigger violent confrontation.

Meanwhile uncertainty, while creating order, can also be a force in subverting order. A degree-zero sociality phase and a phase in which sociality has come to a standstill are both states colored with uncertainty, and in this sense both are forces in establishing order.

In this chapter, I shall discuss the phase of sociality at a standstill and examine how order is established. As part of this examination, I shall reconsider the issue of the scapegoat, touched on in chapter 3, and consider the validity of the proposition that the exertion of violence is a trigger for establishing order.

It is not possible to confirm whether many of the myths collected by Western anthropologists involve scapegoats, and as a result even the interpretations of myths are often arbitrary. In contrast, Kunio Yanagida's *Tōno monogatari* (Tōno folklore) contains anecdotes which clearly involve scapegoats. One example is the story of a man called Tokuya who, during a flood, asks the river deity to change the direction of the flow of the river in exchange for his daughter (Yanagida 1989). The river deity averts disaster, but Tokuya must now offer his daughter as sacrifice in order to repay the deity for his beneficence. In this case the definition of a scapegoat would be one that is intentionally killed as an offering in exchange for some form of benefit from a spiritual being.

In other examples, there is no intention to create a victim, but because no deity exists, someone is killed so that he/she can become the deity. The following story is such an example.

> A priestess found a husband for her only daughter but she did not like the man and was waiting for an opportunity to do something about it. Around the same time, the villagers approached the priestess for a solution to the problem of the entrance to the water supply inlet which collapsed every year. The priestess responded by telling the villagers that someone dressed in white and riding a white horse would pass through the village at dawn in two days time and that they should capture him and get him to become the deity of the dam by burying him at the entrance to the dam. Two days later, the priestess told her son-in-law dress to dress in white clothing, put him on a white horse and sent him on an errand. When a person fitting the description given by the priestess passed through the village, the villagers asked the man to become the deity of the dam. The husband readily accepted their request because it was a message from God but told the villagers that any human sacrifice involved the sacrifice of a couple, and so called for his wife, and the two drowned themselves. At that moment thunder roared and this was followed by three days and three nights of heavy rain. When the water receded, a large rock at the entrance to the dam appeared, and this was then used as a foothold in the construction of a new entrance to the dam. The couple was worshipped as deities of the dam and an annual festival continues to be held today. The grieving priestess, who had unintentionally killed her own daughter, also drowned herself in the same location, and Bonari M*y*ōjin shrine is dedicated to this priestess (Yanagida 1989: 85–6).

The priestess who appears in this story is a powerful figure with the ability to receive divine revelations and pass them onto the villagers, but instead uses her powers to intentionally deceive her son-in-law and the villagers. In this sense, the priestess represents a classical example of a moral conman, or in this case, conwoman.

What enables the priestess' 'con' is the uncertainty generated by the flood. The villagers search for a reason for and solution to this uncertainty. The solution that is chosen is to use violence to create a god, a 'deity.' The villagers are already aware of the option of human sacrifice, and the priestess provides the villagers with a prescription reflecting this (that human sacrifice is one way of overcoming a crisis). The priestess responds to the villagers' request by telling them that 'someone dressed in white and riding a white horse will pass through the village at dawn in two days time. Capture him and make him the deity of the dam by getting him to drown himself at the entrance to the dam'. Anyone other than the villagers would have realized that the priestess' response was nothing other than a validation of murder. The villagers, however, do not recognize this and agree readily, accepting her instructions as the right thing to do. Meanwhile, the priestess' desire to kill her son-in-law is realized in the name of justice for the village (Ogino 1998: 16–8).

Two things are revealed by this story; firstly, that justice for the village is realized through violence, and secondly, that the use of violence in order to realize justice is the result of an arbitrary decision made by someone with power. In other words, the argument proposed by Western social theorists to date – that order was established through the exertion and then the concealment of violence – can arguably be confirmed.

The order of recollection

However, it is important to clarify the type of social order that creates the scapegoat.

The villagers believe the priestess' oracle to be true because she is a mediator who is able to communicate with the gods and the spirits of the dead. Order in the village is sustained by their memories of the dead (their ancestors) who dwell in a sacred place. Thus in the event of an incident, the villagers must ask the spirits of the dead for assistance. I shall therefore refer to the establishment of order through the recollection of the dead as 'the order of recollection' (Ogino 1998, 2002).

In the order of recollection there is an attempt to restore order and overcome a crisis, by arriving at an understanding of the cause of the crisis by relating it to gods and spirits. A crisis could be a natural disaster such as a flood, or a deterioration of social order triggered by a crime such as theft.

Tōno monogatari contains a typical anecdote that demonstrates how the recollection of order functions when a theft takes place.

> In the event of an adversity such as theft, the villagers call on the powers of a god named *mitsuminesama* in order to identify the perpetrator. A man called Yoshitaro Sasaki called on the powers of *mitsuminesama* when *watagase* [*kamishimo* ceremonial dress made of cotton] was stolen from his house. All the lights in the house were turned off and the *goshintai*

> [body of god] placed in the *okuzashiki* [innermost room of the house]. Each of the villagers who had gathered in the house then entered the room to pray to *mitsuminesama*. One woman, however, was terrified and refused to enter the room. When the villagers tried to force her into the room, the woman vomited blood and lost consciousness. The villagers therefore concluded that she was the thief. The woman handed over the stolen goods to the villagers that night' (Yanagida 1989: 101–2).

As is clear from this anecdote, the villagers believed that it was *mitsuminesama* and not they themselves who have the ability to solve crimes of theft. Therefore, a series of rituals were carried out in preparation for this, commencing with the welcoming of the *goshintai* by the villagers. This ritual is clearly only carried out 'when there are already several suspects' (Yanagida 1989: 101) and the villagers already have some idea of who is guilty. It should be possible to identify the perpetrator without having to carry out such rituals. However, the act of reconfirming the function of the order of recollection through the ritual of identifying the perpetrator is of more significance to the villagers than simply identifying the perpetrator for the Sasaki family and returning the *watagase* to them.

Although ostracism and scapegoating involves villagers directly exerting violence, violence was indirectly exerted in this example of theft by forcing the female suspect to vomit blood through the act of ritual. The community exerts violence directly or indirectly against those who it believes have caused a deterioration of order. In each case, the violence is understood to be promoted by a god such as *mitsuminesama* or a priestess who has the ability to communicate with the gods. The exertion of violence is therefore validated because of a god or deity who inhabits a space beyond the boundaries of the village, or a priestess who possesses the powers to communicate with the gods. This signifies that the villagers are hierarchizing the world that they live in, including places accessible to any person through to those only accessible to exceptional people or beings.

In a hiearchized world, those who are estranged from everyday village life and do not completely belong to the village can at times be an authoritative figure of that village, while at other times they can be the target of violence by the villagers. The fact that the priestess has links with another realm means that she can communicate with a realm that the villagers can neither access nor know. Because of this, the priestess' words have authority. However, in the anecdote cited earlier, 'The grieving priestess who had unintentionally killed her own daughter also drowned herself in the same location.' In other words, the priestess also dies and is transformed into Bonari Myōjin.

Genji of Tosa is a beggar who lived under a bridge for 30 years because of the goodwill of *Nasu no danna* (Master Nasu). This implies that the village is tolerant enough to accept a beggar. However, a beggar is set up as human sacrifice in one anecdote in *Tōno monogatari* (Yanagida 1989: 84–5). Meanwhile, Kazuhiko Komatsu points out that beggars and non-persons are frequently chosen as scapegoats (Komatsu 1980: 90). Beggars do not fully belong to a village community. In some cases, they leave the village and in this sense are in touch with the world that lies outside the village. And, it is ambiguous figures such as these who become the target of violence.

The aim behind the order of recollection is not simply to assert violence. In the way that the power of the priestess lies in her ability to communicate with the spirits of the dead, it is an order designed to respond to death, something that represents the most uncertain and incomprehensible of states. The order of recollection is the result of man's greatest concern – how to deal with the death of a loved one. In the order of recollection, there is no clean break between family members who have died and those who are living. The dead are seen as protecting the living and ancestors can at times symbolically communicate with the living. For example, the spirits return to *shigan* [the human world] during the *obon* season and therefore the living carry out rituals to receive their ancestors, such as making daily offerings to the *butsudan* [Buddhist altar]. The order based on the recollection of the dead is therefore established through a never-ending exchange between the living and the spirits of their ancestors. Marcel Mauss, who had a deep understanding of this phenomenon, pointed out that 'among the first groups of beings with whom men must have made contacts were the sprits of the dead and the gods' (Mauss 1969: 13). Underpinning the order of recollection is the primordial exchange between the living, the gods and the spirits of the dead. Therefore the ability to demonstrate one's power to communicate with gods becomes a source of control.

What we can see from the above is that violence is not the trigger for the establishment of order, but that it is the recollection of order that actuates the device (the creation of a scapegoat) that in turn enables the exertion of violence in response to a crisis.

Disaster and order in the modern State

In the previous section, the theory that violence is exerted in order to avoid crises such as disasters was discussed. It is clear, however, that putting this theory into practice would be problematic. This is not because the foundation underpinning the order of recollection in which people mourn the death of loved ones and regularly pray to them is threatened, but is due to a reasoning that is different from the order of recollection. As a result, scapegoating does not necessarily take place as soon as disaster strikes. Major disasters always result in a situation of uncertainty, but the solution is different from the solution applied in the order of recollection. This is due to the existence of the State.

As a rule the modern State has a monopoly on the right to exert physical violence. Only national instruments such as the army or the police are permitted to exert violence. Some countries such as the United States recognize the freedom to possess arms, but the principle that violence can only be exerted by the police and army still applies. In exchange for having a monopoly on the right to exert violence, the State must guarantee the safety of its people. If a situation of uncertainty is generated, the State therefore has an obligation to eliminate this uncertainty. In the event of a disaster, for example, the State has a duty to rescue the victims and carry out activities such as restoration work in the affected area. A situation of uncertainty represents a violation of national order and therefore the situation must be eliminated immediately.

The situation of uncertainty triggered by a major disaster is one in which the boundaries between the public and the private are extinguished. In Japan, the public has been represented, since the Meiji Period, by the State or national government and the regional governments under it. The government remained dominant even after World War II and has not relinquished the attitude that it must carry out its obligations to its citizens. Since the end of World War II, however, the government has not unilaterally stepped into private territory. While the government does not allow intervention by the individual, nor does it enter the realm of personal possessions or ownership, continuing to allow relative freedom in the handling of assets. This is what is meant by the strict boundary that lies between the government and the individual.

For example, a disaster removes the boundary that lies between private space – the foundation of creature comforts – and public space (under the direct control of the State and regional governments). The extinguishing of this boundary was evident after the Great Hanshin Earthquake of 1995. I shall now refer to the Great Hanshin Earthquake to examine the situation of uncertainty following the earthquake and how the government restored the nation (Ogino 1999: 326–344).

The information is based on data collected as a result of the following surveys.

1. Questionnaire survey based on individual interviews with Kobe residents after the Earthquake
    - First carried out from 1 August to 19 August 1995 (208 families, 473 individuals)
    - Carried out next from 1 August to 31 August 1996 (271 families, 834 individuals[2])
2. Interview survey on employees of Kobe City (seven employees), Nishinomiya City, Takarazuka City and Hyogo Prefecture (one each) (who were heavily involved in disaster recovery)
    - Eight individuals from October to November 1995 (based on group interviews)
    - Two individuals in November 1996 (based on group interviews)
3. Individual interviews with the Director of Temporary Housing Association and one other (two persons), May 1996

Let us first examine the statement by a 42-year old female victim (receptionist at an orthopedic clinic) from Nada Ward in Kobe City. Her story clearly conveys the uncertainty that prevailed after the earthquake.

> Someone deliberately lit a fire near the evacuation site the day after the earthquake and so we all fled to the park. I helped carry dead bodies with no idea of who they were. The bodies were so heavy that I ended up leaving them in the middle of the road and we somehow managed to escape. We spent the night in a park in temperatures below zero and I ended up catching a cold. (abbreviated) The bodies stored in the classroom began to decompose and we were asked to place dry ice inside, even though there were no coffins. People from a company in Osaka came and took the bodies away at great expense…

It is unclear as to whether the fire really was 'deliberately lit.' However, what is clear is that this woman was forced into a situation in which she had to live in government or public facilities such as a classroom and a park – places that came under the jurisdiction of the local government – which had been transformed into refuges, and moreover, that the woman even assisted in carrying the bodies that she found lying beside her. After this, the woman began living (from the end of July) in the public facility of temporary housing with her family (her husband and two children).

The next statement is from a 26-year old male victim from Suma Ward.

> The parents of my younger sister's fiancée from Higashi Nada were killed during the earthquake. The local fire brigade removed their bodies from the rubble. Although both the fire brigade and police arrived at the scene, nobody took the bodies away because they didn't have the right equipment. I went to the Ward office and was told that we should obtain this equipment and transport the bodies ourselves, which was impossible because of the conditions of the roads. In the end, we placed the bodies in the family car for the night and moved them to the primary school ourselves the following day.

This man was frustrated because neither the fire brigade, the police nor the ward office assisted him. He believed that the site of an accident or disaster should be dealt with by the government. A disaster site is a public space and under normal circumstances residents would not be able to enter this space. And yet, when the fire brigade and the police arrived, they did not carry out their duties. This is the sort of situation in which the boundary that lies between the public and the private is extinguished. There are many other examples of this sort of extinguishment of the boundary between the public and the private. Life in a refuge – where one's private life is carried out in a public space – and life in temporary housing are both examples in which the boundary between the public and the private has been extinguished. Some people were even forced to sleep outdoors because they were unable to get into refuges. The following statement is by a 70-year old male victim from Nada Ward.

> I was buried in rubble for two and a half hours. The refuges were all full. There wasn't even any standing room in both the gymnasium and the classrooms. Only elderly women were allowed into the refuges and so I lit a fire in a vacant block of land near my house and spent the night there. Later someone from a funeral parlor lent me a tent. There was a

procession of bodies being carried away. Four families lived in a single tent (until mid-March).

What is evident from the above statements is that the state in which the boundaries between the public and the private have disappeared represents sociality at a standstill, and can be compared to the 'natural state' expounded by social theorists since Hobbes. The situation immediately after the earthquake was as though people suddenly found themselves in an 'uncivilized' time in history.

As Hobbes argued, in the natural state, the concept of private ownership either does not exist or has disappeared. As a result, people are controlled by their fear of theft or violence. Hobbes pointed out that 'Force and fraud are in war (= natural state) the two cardinal virtues.' The sense of fear felt amongst the victims of the earthquake is clearly expressed by the following statement.

> My house was destroyed and I walked out of the house with nothing. All I could manage was to grab some socks through the window and so I was wearing five layers of socks and standing in front of the house. A man in his thirties approached me and asked me how much I would pay him to get anything I wanted from the ruins of my house (Abreviated). In the end my jewellery and share certificates which were in a snakeskin bag went missing. All my jewellery was stolen. Even my pots went missing. I had nothing. My son arrived in the morning with a shovel thinking that we had been killed and took me back to his house. I paid him 50,000 yen as rent and continued to pay for food for the entire family but we ended up arguing after about a month and I had to move out. For the next six months I was constantly on the move, staying with my daughter or with relatives.
>
> Every day I'd carry my backpack and make the rounds of all the real estate agents in Ashiya and Myodani. I searched for five months and finally managed to find the apartment we're living in now, but I worry about how many more years we can stay here with the rent at 100,000 yen. I've applied numerous times for temporary or government housing but was unsuccessful. But I'm collecting the rejection postcards that I've received. I heard that you get priority if you have more than three of these postcards. I'm avoiding Nishi Ward because I want to be near my husband's work and the hospital that I go to regularly.
>
> I'm diabetic and without insulin I'd have an episode and not be able to breathe. I was really lucky because I managed to get some sweets from the kiosk at the train station immediately after the earthquake. Other

> diabetics use insulin derived from pig or cow pancreas but I use insulin derived from humans. It's a special type of insulin which costs around 10,000 yen a bottle and you can only get it at my usual hospital. At one stage the hospital closed down and so I went to a hospital in Ashiya to get the insulin but it was absolute chaos there. I felt so desperate (65-year old housewife from Chuo Ward, Kobe).

Strangers can not be trusted in situations such as these. Even one's neighbors only think about themselves. People complained about their next-door neighbors who were rescued first and who, despite knowing that there were others who had also buried been alive, did not bother informing the rescue workers. Many were shocked at the transformation in people that they had once respected. Many victims found themselves in situations immediately after the earthquake in which they questioned good and evil. The following is a statement by a 40 year old male (yoga teacher) from Chuo Ward:

> There was a clear distinction between the good and the bad. Some people were extremely helpful, there were many volunteers and I could see that there were many good people. But I also saw people stealing from burnt-out sites, overcharging of food, and the greed of people in the building industry.

As expressed by the words 'people stealing from burnt-out sites, over-charging of food, and the greed of people in the building industry', this man felt that the situation that was created was, to quote Hobbes, one in which 'manipulation' was a virtue. There are countless statements of lies, deceit, mendaciousness and fraudulent acts. A 52-year old woman (whose home was completely destroyed) who ran a Chinese restaurant spoke as she watched customers entering her premises.

> Tradesmen seem to be doing well and come here to drink beer in the middle of the day. They say they only have to work four hours because they're earning 80,000 yen a day. That's because tradesmen from Kobe go to Nagoya, register their addresses there and then work here, charging extra for transportation and accommodation. Someone living in a refuge told me that her husband's been transferred to another city and because she's on her own and her son's in high school, she's been working, earning 300,000 yen a month. She told me that she'll manage to save quite a bit in two years, and I' m sure she will!

A Kobe City employee made the following statement about applications for temporary housing.

> Quite a few people lie when they apply for temporary housing, in particular by claiming that there's someone with a disability in their family when there isn't. If I ask to see their disability book, they say they don't have one. They tell me that they don't have a disability book but that the family member definitely has a disability.

Some applicants who were offered temporary housing did not actually move in.

> Around 10% use temporary housing for storage and only turn up when emergency rations are distributed. I'm assuming that the people living in other temporary housing lets them know. We ask the government to provide the addresses of these people but they refuse to do so. I've heard that some people are even subletting their homes. The people living in temporary housing are supposed to be elderly women who are 65 or 70 years old, but there are young people living in there (Director of the Temporary Housing Association).

Another Kobe City employee pointed out that some people had moved their belongings into temporary housing but weren't actually living there. He acknowledged that people who were allocated temporary housing were in fact not moving in so that the houses remained vacant. According to this employee, one of the City's measures to deal with this situation is to put up a notice, remove the belongings from the house and make the place available to the next person. However, not once did government authorities intervene. Indeed, according to one testimony, 'the water pipe of a house that should have been occupied but was in fact vacant (the resident a 'ghost victim') burst, and the pipe was repaired immediately because it was the home of the Assistant General Secretary of the Diet Members Support Group.'

In these ways, many people tried to benefit as much as possible from a situation of uncertainty in which the boundaries between the public and the private were extinguished. There were those who tried to pass themselves off as being worse off than genuine victims, altering their authorized 'extent of destruction' form from 'partially destroyed' to 'semi-destroyed' or from 'semi-destroyed to 'totally destroyed.' (According to a Kobe City employee) others received 20 or

30 rationed meals each per day. The list was endless. One government employee expressed his frustration.

> Many of the people who approached the government expressed their dissatisfaction at what was available. For example, despite the fact that the condition for entering temporary housing was that you had to be age 60 or over, a 59-year-old person would ask why he couldn't move into the nearby temporary housing that remained unoccupied. The vacancies are due to the fact that 30% of the applicants later withdrew their applications, but it wouldn't be fair to others if we were to bend the rules.

From the government's point of view, a situation of uncertainty that allows anyone to become a scam artist is unacceptable (according to one Kobe City employee, during the month following the earthquake, the government's chain of command was so ambiguous that people were forced to make their own decisions). This is because it is no longer possible to guarantee certainty in life in such a situation. Therefore, in the way that those who could not achieve self-reliance in Western society in the 19th Century were assisted to become 'individuals' (refer chapter 1), the State also assists disaster victims to become self-reliant. Another reason to avoid a state of uncertainty that may give way for scam artists is to quickly overcome the instability of order – something unacceptable to the State – by providing relief to the disaster victims.

The State establishes a budget for providing relief to the disaster victims. Another interpretation would be that the State has a monopoly in the right to execute the budget to provide relief to the victims and to restore the situation. As a result, the State can exert its authority through the provision of benefits. If the premise behind this is the self-reliance of the individual, then the government application process represents an exceptional act. As a result, the government contact office becomes a judging agency that determines whether the application is valid or invalid, and only the applications recognized as being essential to the individual's self-reliance are accepted. The government establishes rules to eliminate any fraudulent applications and this is seen as being 'fair.' A Kobe City employee made the following statement.

> The government is all about applications based on the principle of achieving self-reliance. But it's difficult to determine whether applicants really require assistance, whether they simply think they may as well

> apply, or whether they're just regular troublemakers. I dealt with these applicants after the earthquake and in the end I wasn't able to identify which category they belonged to.

As is evident from this statement, government departments dislike 'troublemakers' and believe that eliminating these types as much as possible represents justice. The government is attempting to establish justice by attempting to eliminate conmen. This is because the modern State is based on an 'anti-fraud philosophy', and as referred to in chapter 1, the modern State has established a system in which fraud is policed by law enforcement. Both the central government and local governments are centers of investigation for eliminating fraud, and government officials are qualified to carry out such investigations.

A similar logic is applied to the qualifications of professionals such as judges, lawyers, doctors and teachers. A characteristic of these specialist professions is that they are qualified to record personal facts, an essential part of establishing individualism. Not anyone is allowed to keep records. Only a small number of people are permitted to do so and their ability to do so is recognized by the State. In other words, the modern State was established through the establishment of a national system of accreditation of 'recorders' such as judges and doctors. Pascal bemoaned the 'fraudulent' nature of judges and doctors[3], but the modern State attempted to guarantee the validity of specialist professions by systematizing doctors' licences and bar exams.

One example is snake doctors who were perceived as a problem in France from around the 18th Century (Sato 1994: 23–33). Swiss physician Tissot condemned snake doctors, claiming that they represented 'the biggest plague in medicine.' Snake doctors are 'folk medicine practitioners' who have not studied medicine at a University and who have no specialist medical knowledge.

However, social history research into medicine in 18th Century France reveals that there was no significant difference between 'doctors with qualifications' and 'snake doctors.' Patients did not necessarily always prefer a qualified doctor over a snake doctor – as far as patients were concerned, they had a choice. As though reflecting Pascal's cynical depiction of doctors as questionable and phony, there was no real difference in ability between a qualified doctor and an unqualified doctor and if anything, there was a greater demand for snake doctors. This was because the snake doctor was confident in his or her dealings with the patient and offered individualized treatment for each patient. According to Noriko Sato, the snake doctor 'treated the patient as a whole and addressed each patient individually' and 'provided holistic treatment.' This lack of clear boundaries between the legitimate doctor and the snake doctor was gradually eliminated with the establishment of medical departments at universities during the 19th Century. It became illegal to provide medical treatment without qualifications, and folk remedies went into decline. The State took on the role of treating diseases – typically contagious diseases – that generated uncertainty and also took on the role of preventing these diseases. Medical education was provided towards the realization of this system and medical qualifications became a national qualification.

Interestingly, however, the establishment of boundaries between the scam artist and the specialist did not result in the elimination of fraud. Indeed it created an environment that allowed the proliferation of scam artists and conmen. Frank Abagnale describes his experience as a conman in *Catch Me If You Can*. Abagnale passed himself off as a pilot, a doctor and a lawyer, and even went as far as teaching a summer intensive course at university. After the end of the intensive course, 'at least fifty students stopped me on my way out and told me how much they enjoyed the course and bid me farewell' (Abagnale 1980). As this anecdote comes from an ex-conman, we can not be sure of its reliability, but positions of doctor, lawyer and pilot were aspired to, and provided ideal fodder with which the conman could spin his tale. Fraud continues unabated because a system was established that made fraud illegal.

Traditional society and modern society

The modern State has a monopoly on the right to exert violence, but because it is governed by law, it can not formally exert arbitrary violence. The premise for the monopoly for the exertion of violence is that the State is the source of justice. Therefore, the State is infallible. Because the underlying principle is that the exertion of violence is justified, even when violence is being exerted it is not seen recognized as such, as illustrated in the example of Mito Kōmon who is integrated into the world that he establishes[4]. Indeed, it must not be seen that violence is being exerted.

In reality, however, the State ensures that its instruments exert violence in situations in which sociality has come to a standstill. Alternatively, the State creates a 'supra-legal situation' whereby sociality is intentionally made to come to a standstill. In the majority of cases this is concealed, thereby generating national conspiracy theories. Examples include the Shimoyama Incident which took place in post-war Japan, and the assassination of John F. Kennedy in the United States, both of which remain shrouded in mystery today. General Aussaresses is a rare example of someone actually confessing to exerting violence.

General Aussaresses claimed that he tortured and massacred independence activists in Algeria, then a French colony, between 1955 and 1957 where he was a secret agent. He later went on to publish his story. The following is a description of the first time that Aussaresses tortured a prisoner.

> The man wouldn't talk and so I decided to be more extreme. I somehow managed it without the help of the police. It was the first time I'd tortured someone, but the torture wasn't productive, because the man died without giving up any information. I didn't think anything of it. I didn't feel any regret that the man had died. My one regret was that I'd allowed the man to die before extracting information from him' (Aussaresses 2001).

After this incident, Aussaresses went on to kill countless independence activists and collaborators.

> The arrestees were tortured at night, but few survived by morning. They were all killed in the end, whether they gave up information or not' (Aussaresses 2001).

According to Aussaresses, this indiscriminate murder was not the intention of the individual but the 'State's intention.'

> When we found ourselves having to kill arrestees, (abbreviated) we never once doubted that we were simply following the orders of the French Republic. (abbreviated) Torture was tolerated and indeed was encouraged (Abbreviated). The methods I employed were always the same – beating, electric shock and water torture. The last method was the most dangerous to the arrestee' (Aussaresses 2001).

Francois Mitterand, Minister for Justice at the time (and later President), was aware that torture was being practiced, but this fact was covered up and as a result not legally pursued.

In his memoirs, Aussaresses' asserts unequivocably that massacre and torture were carried out to protect the nation of France. The State, in order to protect itself, exerts violence without legitimate procedures in place and then conceals the facts of the matter. Aussaresse (and policymakers at the time) saw this as legitimate and believed that these acts were necessary in order to maintain order.

Aussaresse's story is not a myth but historical testimony. In this sense, there is a difference in the way the exertion of violence is recognized and expressed between the world depicted in *Tōno monogatari*, and that of the French Republic for which Aussaresse served as an agent. Unlike the world depicted in *Tōno monogatari*, violence is not exerted arbitrarily in the modern State, while Norbert Elias argues that there is a significant reduction in opportunities for physical violence to be exerted on an everyday level in the modern State. According to Elias (Elias 1969), people living in Medieval Europe were rude, shameless, quick to express their emotions and often resorted to violence. It took centuries for people to become civilized and able to reflect on their actions and behave appropriately. It was the modern State that promoted civilization. It was because the State monopolized the right to exert violence that the individual lost his/her opportunity to exert violence him/herself, resulting in the suppression of the aggressive instinct. The result was a civilized society which was different in every way from a violent society.

However, were the people who lived in the Middle Ages really so emotional and rude in comparison to people who live in the Modern Era? If, hypothetically speaking, people living in medieval times were savages, then one can argue that this was because people during the Middle Ages were not sufficiently socialized. Socialization signifies the existence of various norms in everyday life which people have assimilated into their lives. According to the theory of civilization, few such norms existed during the Middle Ages as they do in civilized society, and therefore people acted savagely. However, the theory that society progresses to become increasingly civilized has been 'betrayed' by the reality of the massacre of Jews at the hands of the Nazis in Germany, Elias' birthland. In fact, it is because the modern State has a monopoly on the right to exert violence that the exertion of arbitrary violence becomes possible.

As questioning the validity of this argument would provide no conclusion, I would like to make just one obvious point. Even if, hypothetically speaking, people living in the Middle Ages were emotional and violent, this is only because they appear that way from modern man's perspective. Medieval man would not see his own behavior as particularly irrational. If medieval man knew of the reality of war during the 20th Century, he could well believe that it represented a much more violent time than the Middle Ages. A belief in the possibility of a shift from savagery to civilization through a historical process is nothing more than one value judgment. It can not, however, be verified.

If anything, the following description is more appropriate: People represent a combination of characteristics and can at times be emotional, aggressive or violent. If these characteristics erupt because they are not kept under control and this behavior is defined as unsocial, then arguably people can, at times, have a predilection for unsocial behavior. Violence is a human mode of existence predating socialization. In this sense, a fundamental mode of existence predates the classification of society into 'traditional' society and 'modern' society. In comparison to this, the classification of society in to 'traditional' and 'modern' is arguably superficial. There are, however, several differences. One is, as has frequently been pointed out in this book, whether there is an attempt to present the facts – whether there is a focus on differentiating between what is true and false. The more one tries to differentiate between what is true and false, the more zero-degree sociality is eliminated. This is because the differentiation of what is true and false is irrelevant in the degree-zero sociality phase. Whether a certain act is fraudulent, or is in fact a proof of friendship, is unclear in this phase, and the meaning of the act is yet to be established. However, it is in the degree-zero sociality phase that a creation of a 'place', that encourages one to tune-in to another in response to an approach, is promoted. This tuning-in takes the form of gift-giving. The act of gift-giving means that the tuning-in process that takes place in the degree-zero sociality is then transformed into collaborativity.

Let us consider fraud or the con once again. Tuning-in to the conman begins with gift-giving. Handing over money to the conman represents nothing other than an act of gift-giving. The next chapter examines, in detail, how gift-giving is linked to the establishment of collaborativity.

5 The Intention to Give Gifts

Gift-giving and exchange

Why does one give money to another? Knowing that there is little possibility that the money will be returned, why is one prepared to relinquish one's own money? Do people have an intrinsic desire to give? Do people knowingly become deceived?

In anthropology since Mauss, gift-giving has been discussed from the perspective that it provides an opportunity for exchange. According to Mauss, in 'an uncivilized society' intertribal networks are established through the exchange of rare items. Moreover, as can be seen in *kula*[1] exchange, the exchanged items are not allowed to remain in one's possession for longer than a prescribed period of time. There is also an obligation to give a gift in return, thereby creating a social obligation or 'duty' that, once embarked on, can not be ended. Gift-giving therefore creates the three 'obligations' of 'giving', 'receiving' and 'returning.' When one is presented with a gift, that gift can not be refused and must eventually be reciprocated with the addition of 'interest', and this process must be repeated over and over again.

According to Lévi-Strauss, who was inspired by Mauss' *Gift* (Lévi-Strauss 1978), communication based on exchange is fundamental to human behavior and, although involving risk, still remains the only strategy for communicating with others. Lévi-Strauss explains this phenomenon by citing, as an example, an unremarkable scene – the behavior of two strangers who happened to sit next to each other in a restaurant in the South of France. Unlike the Japanese, the French spend time over their meal, even when eating in a cheap café. It would therefore be quite a challenge for two strangers seated next to each other not to exchange a few words during their meal. 'This is the fleeting but difficult situation resolved by the exchanging of wine' (Lévi-Strauss 1969: 59). The two men do not simply drink the wine that always comes with the meal: by one offering wine to the other seated beside him, an opportunity is created to speak, thereby bridging the gap between the two strangers. In this sense, the wine represents a form of 'public property.'

Lévi-Strauss recognizes the traces of a 'fundamental situation' in the scene in the restaurant in the South of France. This is the same situation that uncivilized people or groups find themselves in when they come into contact with strangers for the first time. Hunting peoples exchange their women in the same way that they exchange their quarry. In exchange for giving 'them' our women, their women are given to 'us.' This represents an exchange of equivalents. According to Lévi-Strauss, 'The role (of exchange) in primitive society is essential because it embraces material objects, social values and women' (Lévi-Strauss 1969: 62).

Lévi-Strauss emphasizes the fact that people tend towards exchange, even in confrontation. People can not tolerate isolation and find themselves almost unconsciously giving gifts. The giving away of women through marriage, too, is nothing more than the first step in the larger process of gift-giving that follows.

Mauss and Lévi-Strauss proposed that 'gift-giving creates exchange.' Derrida, however, makes the following comment about Mauss' *Gift*.

> One could go so far as to say that a work as monumental as Marcel Mauss's *The Gift*[14] speaks of everything but the gift: It deals with economy, exchange, contract (*do ut des*), it speaks of raising the stakes, sacrifice, gift *and* countergift – in short, everything that in the thing itself impels the gift *and* the annulment of the gift (Derrida 1992: 24).

For Derrida, the gift-giving that creates a cycle of exchange does not represent gift-giving as such. A gift must, in essence, be something that is forgotten by the two parties so that this cycle of exchange is not created. In this sense, Derrida argues that gift-giving is impossible (it is impossible for the parties involved to be aware of it). Certainly, giving a gift to someone is not carried out with the anticipation of it being reciprocated. If anything, in an act of pure gift-giving, 'reciprocation' would be refused. There is no need for either the person giving the gift or the person receiving that gift to interpret the act as creating an 'exchange.' There is no need for the person receiving the gift to feel a sense of obligation that he/she should reciprocate.

It is important at this point to recall the Ashikaga Bank Embezzlement. Abe, the conman, set up a company of which he was president – International Union Development Center – with the money that he received from Ōbayashi . This company was in the prime location of Nishi Azabu in Minato Ward, Tokyo. The office 'featured bright green wall-to-wall carpet and quality desks and chairs, giving the impression that this was a company doing a lot of business, a company on the rise' (*Shūkan Asahi* magazine, 8 August 1975 issue). The aim of the company was 'to gather and provide information on horseracing' and employed around 40 people. The employees were always paid on time, and their monthly pay – the senior managing director's salary being 180,000 yen and female, high-school graduate employees' salary being 100,000 yen – was above average for the time (1975). However, although the company claimed that it gathered and provided information on horseracing, it was not the employees who were gathering this information. Abe simply signed up with another forecasting company that provided information and his company simply passed this information on to its clients. As there was no way that Abe's company could have turned a profit under these conditions, the employees' wages and the rent for the building were paid for with the funds obtained from the Ashikaga Bank via Ōbayashi . According to *Shūkan Shinchō* magazine's 7 August 1975 issue, 'it's an ideal workplace for young Japanese who don't like working, because all they have to do is spend the day in a flashy building, sitting around in luxury chairs without any mental or physical exertion and yet still getting paid.'

One employee made the following comment about Abe, the company president.

> Mr Abe would say some surprising things. He once told us that he was a conman. He spoke in riddles – at one meeting he told us that lying's fine as long as you make the lie not a lie. (Abbreviated) He often told us how people made their money, and he told us that he'd studied at four different universities and that he was once a struggling student living in a two-tatami [3 square-meter] room (7 August 1975 issue, *Shūkan Shinchō* magazine).

The very fact that Abe admitted to being a conman is of interest, but even more interesting is the following observation in *Shūkan Shinchō* magazine's 28 August 1975 issue.

> More puzzling is what exactly a 25 year-old man with a criminal record for burglary was thinking when he set up a company, employed 40 employees and continued to pay their wages. He could have easily kept

> the 200 million yen that he talked his lover into procuring for him. Did he really think that a company with so many employees could make a profit through the dodgy business of providing horserace forecasting services or selling wreaths bearing the names of celebrities?

In court Ōbayashi, who had given 200 million yen to Abe over a two year period, would only say that she did not know why she gave him the money but that she was definitely attracted to him (Sawachi 1976). Even stranger than the fact that Ōbayashi gave money to Abe is that Abe had set up a company. According to *Shūkan Shinchō* magazine, although Abe 'had serious intentions of succeeding as an entrepreneur' there was obviously no need for him to set up a company. Indeed, the fact that he personally continued to pay the wages (with the funds Ōbayashi was handing over to Abe) – as the company was not making any profit – of as many as 40 employees who were not doing any kind of real work, can also be interpreted as Abe simply giving money to his employees in the form of wages.

Abe was obviously unaware that he was giving money away to his employees. Neither Ōbayashi nor Abe saw this act of giving as something that should be reciprocated. They were simply handing over their money, and paradoxically, this represents the essence of gift-giving as defined by Derrida and represents gift-giving that the parties involved did not recognize as such: a pure form of gift-giving. Moreover, the structure of this gift-giving is the exact opposite to the structure represented by the labor relationship within a capitalist system.

In capitalism, one's labor is compensated for in the form of wages. Clearly, therefore, wages do not represent a gift. Karl Marx, an opponent of market economics, believed that the capitalist and the worker are not, in reality, equals. This is because, according to Marxist theory, the capitalist engages in capitalist production through the exploitation of the worker by appropriating part of the value of what the worker produces. In other words the worker is giving part of the value (product) that he creates to the capitalist, but the worker (and the capitalist) is not aware of this.

However, the International Union Development Center, established by Abe, did not exploit its workers. Indeed, the company continued to be committed to paying its employees who were doing little work. There was no equivalent exchange between the company and the workers, nor were the workers exploited. The company was simply engaged in pure gift-giving.

Gift exchange and product exchange

Mauss tended to see gift-giving and gift-exchange as the same thing. However, as we have seen in the previous section, gift-giving does not include expectations of reciprocation and therefore gift-giving does not necessarily create exchange. In other words, there are two types of giving; pure gift-giving in which there is no expectation of reciprocation, and gift exchange, in which the gift-giving represents a trigger for exchange.

The latter does not represent equivalent exchange. Of the gift giver and the gift recipient, it is the gift giver that is in a superior position. This is because the recipient is obliged to reciprocate. The exchange of gifts creates an imbalance between the parties involved in the exchange, and is significantly different from the equivalent exchange that is the model for market economics. We can see that the market economics model is realized by either negating or ignoring the theory of gift exchange.

Moreover, as seen in chapter 1, in a market economy, people behave in a way that will guarantee certainty in life. This is because the premise is that (1) wealth is scarce and (2) acquired resources become the individual's property. It is based on this premise that the individual works towards securing personal wealth. Paul Samuelson, in his textbook *Economics*, argues that wealth must be produced and appropriately distributed because resources are limited. If resources were unlimited, there would be no need to consider 'economics.' Hobbes believed that people compete, become involved in conflicts, and confront each other, over scarce goods or resources. This violent view of the world– that conflict is generated over the scarcity of goods or resources – has underpinned economics since Hobbes, and the premise of the economics of scarcity originates in this violent, Hobbesian view.

Mauss's *Gift* attempts to overturn this myth of scarcity. He argues that if gift exchange is fundamental to society and therefore gift-giving represents the most valuable of acts, the retention of wealth instead of giving it away represents a negative act.

Of the anthropologists since Mauss, it is Marshall Sahlins who criticizes economics based on the myth of scarcity, arguing that uncivilized society is essentially an affluent society. Because it is affluent, the working hours are limited (Sahlins 1981). Sahlins uses anthropological data to argue that the myth of scarcity is nothing other than a capitalist myth.

Meanwhile, Paul Dumouchel argues that the principle of the myth of scarcity is theoretically doubtful (Dupuy et Dumouchel 1979). In economics as represented by Samuelson, production is carried out in order to fulfill human demand. In other words, demand provides the impetus for production. However, increased productivity intensifies consumption demand (Samuelson 1970). In other words, production stimulates (creates) consumption demand. When one considers the basic principle of economics, it is evident that this poses a problem of whether it is production or demand that comes first.

Moreover, if production creates new demand, then this means that the economic aim of satisfying demand can never be achieved. If the aim of a capitalist economy is to constantly create new demand through production, then demand can never be completely satisfied. It is Dumouchel's argument that the myth of scarcity has in fact been created by capitalist economics and that it is this myth that provides the impetus for capitalism.

The primary aim of capitalism is the pursuit of wealth. However, in societies in which priority is given to gift exchange, 'If one hoards, it is only to spend later on, to put people under obligation and to win followers' (Mauss 1979: 73).

Exchange and violence

If a gift has to be reciprocated, then an exchange becomes an act of 'provocation' by giving someone a gift that can not possibly be reciprocated. In other words, gift-giving also has the potential for violence. It is this aspect that Mauss was probably most interested in. Mauss makes the following observation about this aspect of gift-giving in *The Gift*.

> (With *potlach*) sometimes there is no question of receiving return; one destroys simply in order to give the appearance that one has no desire to receive anything back (abbreviated) to level and crush a rival (Mauss 1979: 35).

This is a form of gift-giving that Mauss coined 'antagonistic (agonistique)' and in which he referred to the American Indian custom called *potlatch*. To 'destroy' in order to 'crush a rival' is based on the principle that a gift must be reciprocated with a gift of greater value.

The statement 'one destroys simply in order to give the appearance that one has no desire to receive anything back' brings to mind the South American Tupi-Guarani tribe. One of the conditions of becoming a Tupi-Guarani tribal chief is to generously share one's wealth with other members of the tribe. The result is that the tribal chief ends up being the poorest member of the tribe (Clastres 1974). Leaving aside the issue of the accuracy of Clastres' observation, those who exert authority must be the 'civil servants' who do not serve their own self-interest.

Gift-giving can therefore be used to attain power, while gift-giving can also be practiced by one who has acquired wealth over a short time, in order to evade jealousy and envy of others or to convey his importance in the community; this can also be seen in contemporary society.

For example, the IT millionaires who reside in Silicon Valley in the United States are involved in a range of volunteer activities. This can take the form of providing financial assistance to a specific program, or involve physical activity carried out in groups such as cleaning up litter on the beach. These activities are not simply ways of minimizing tax. According to French anthropologist Marc Abeles, these young IT millionaires feel compelled to volunteer or fundraise because of the anxiety they are feeling after suddenly finding themselves possessing extreme wealth.

In the tales of 'becoming possessed' that are raised in folklore, unfortunate things can happen as a result of holding onto wealth, even if that wealth was acquired over a short period of time. A villager who has suddenly attained wealth is rumored to be possessed by a fox, and is consequently unable to marry. The wealthy villager is effectively isolated from the community, and this is how he, who did not share his wealth, is punished. The Silicon Valley IT millionaires might be voluntarily parting with their wealth to avoid similar social sanctions.

It is clear from the above that gift-giving includes situations in which people voluntarily part with their wealth (1) in an attempt to attain power through the act of gift-giving or (2) out of fear of holding onto their wealth and thereby attracting envy and jealousy within the community. This represents gift-giving to crush a rival or to avoid being attacked by others. This indicates the possibility of violent confrontation if the gift is rejected. From the perspective of Mauss' principle of exchange, the refusal of exchange triggered by gift-giving is not only generated by the recipient but also by the giver of the gift because the gift giver has not fulfilled his/her obligations. When seen from the perspective that violence is generated when a gift is refused, this enables a redefinition of the source of violence. This view first emerged in Lévi-Strauss' anthropology.

As we have seen earlier, according to Lévi-Strauss, people offer and receive gifts because they can not endure remaining strangers. The act of giving is not necessarily risk-free, however, as there is always the possibility that the gift will be rejected. Lévi-Strauss, in his little-known thesis *Guerre et commerce chez les Indiens de l'Amerique du Sud*, points out that 'commercial transactions represent potential ways of peacefully resolving wars, and wars are the result of unsuccessful transactions' (Lévi-Strauss 1943: 136). A similar argument is made in Lévi-Strauss' major work, *The Elementary Structures of Kinship*:

> There is a link, a continuity, between hostile relations and the provision of reciprocal prestations. Exchanges are peacefully resolved wars, and wars are the result of unsuccessful transactions (Lévi-Strauss 1969: 67).

Although the term 'commerce' is used in *Guerre et commerce chez les Indiens de l'Amerique du Sud*, this has been replaced by 'exchange' in *The Elementary Structures of Kinship*, and not economic exchange, but the exchange of gifts. Other than this, however, there is little difference in the argument developed in both works. In both examples, Lévi-Strauss points out that there is a fine line between war and exchange.

The strategy of establishing exchange and then waiting for an opportunity to wield control (to try and ensure that the other party can not reciprocate the gift) is enabled when there is an understanding that an act of gift-giving creates a cycle of exchange. A tacit rule or a sense of trust that has not yet been regularized (or the tuned-in relationship referred to in this book) must have been established for this cycle to begin. There is, however, always the possibility of rules being broken, of trust being betrayed. There is always the possibility that the gift will be refused, and it is when this happens that violence such as war is generated.

There is also the potential for violence when one party decides that a fair exchange has not been carried out. The violence is not necessarily exerted by this deceived party. If anything, in most cases it is the deceiver or the perpetrator of fraud who exerts violence, either after being condemned for the unfair exchange or in fear of it becoming an issue. This is clearly demonstrated by the incidence of people who commit murder after their con or scam has been revealed.

From the above, therefore, one can argue that violence is generated when the gift-giving or exchange has failed. This argument questions the view of the 'violent person' as represented by Hobbes. These persons that Hobbes had in mind were those who, finding themselves isolated in the natural state = state of war, constantly worried about being attacked by the enemy, or 'violent persons' who exert violence from the fear of being attacked.

From this argument emerges the theory that the role of war is to integrate the community. Pierre Clastres criticizes his mentor Lévi-Strauss' theory for the proposition that 'first there was exchange', thereby presenting war in a negative light. Clastres then goes on to argue that war was something that was positive for the community and that uncivilized societies engaged in war to protect their 'autonomy.' Clastres argues that uncivilized society is a society that primarily rejects exchange with others (Clastres 1974).

As we have seen so far, physical and symbolic violence is exerted in order for society to survive. It is true that conflict can be actively carried out in order to maintain society, as argued by Clastres. However, the integration of the community is not a sufficient explanation for why war is generated. This is because it is the view of the community for which the possibilities of gift-giving has been eliminated. Certainly, Lévi-Strauss' view that people eventually move towards gift-giving can be seen as optimistic. However, Lévi-Strauss' statement that 'wars are the result of unsuccessful transactions' is nonetheless important. The exertion of violence is the result of encounters and communication between multiple individuals or organizations – not the result of people waiting and taking advantage of opportunities to exert violence. Similarly, people do not only work hard to protect their wealth but at times give away some of their wealth to others.

The emergence of morals

Pure gift-giving which, according to Derrida, is impossible, can at times be recognized as gift-giving, transformed into exchange and then become convention. It is often at this moment that morals are called for.

Conmen often approach someone with the intention to deceive by appealing to his/her sense of morals as this is the most effective way of extracting money from them. Pyramid selling schemes also utilize strategies that appeal to people's sense of morals. The sales strategy used in pyramid selling schemes first stimulates the sales personnel's desire for upward mobility. A pyramid selling scheme involves the exponential expansion of the organization, with the need for a differentiation between the sales personnel on the top and those at the bottom of the expanding hierarchy. Hearing about the high incomes and prosperous lifestyles of the sales personnel at the top of the pyramid, those at the bottom of the pyramid strive to ascend the pyramid.

The 'Sales Personnel Acquisition Manual' of one pyramid selling scheme outlines various 'persuasive lines' to be used by the 'sales leader' in charge of the 'sales team' to 'acquire' sales personnel. These include lines such as 'Why live a life full of regrets?' and 'Young, rich and driving a great car – a superstar!' According to the manual, it is important to emphasize to potential sales personnel that improving sales can deliver a prosperous lifestyle. It also adds, however, that anyone not registering interest when these 'lines' are delivered should be 'ignored.' A boundary has to be drawn between those interested in making money and those who aren't, so that sales personnel are seduced into thinking that the sales team is made up only of the chosen few. Finally, it advises the supervisor that 'Most importantly, the sales leader must be a person worthy of the title. The sales leader should be knowledgeable and cultivated, with good business skills, good breeding and be kind.' In other words, those at the top must hone one's knowledge and character.

Pyramid selling schemes involve sales personnel purchasing the products and then relying on their skills to sell them on to others. The salesperson therefore sees his/her initial purchase of the products as an 'investment.' Morals are utilized to justify the eagerness to invest. Preaching to sales personnel by expounding virtues that promise new opportunities, such as 'Change your life!' and 'Aim to become a superstar!' has the effect of stimulating eagerness to invest.

What is evident from the example of pyramid selling schemes is that morals are nothing more than a tool of the con or scam for the conman. This demonstrates indirectly that there are no grounds for morality, a point also emphasized in modern social theory.

One view is that power struggles are fundamental, and there is no basis for a normative concept of morality. This is the position taken by Marx and Pascal before him, but as mentioned in chapter 3, it is Bourdieu who presents this argument in modern sociology. Bourdieu believes that power struggles are determined by the type and amount of 'capital' being held. The types of capital include economic capital, social capital (the extent of the human network being maintained), academic capital, and cultural capital.

For example, business executives of major corporations who own a great deal of economic capital, and intelligentsia or artists who own cultural capital are the same in the sense that power struggles take place in both groups, but the capital that can be mobilized is very different. If we were to examine the morals of a business executive and an artist, the former's morals would probably be based on 'work and effort' while some artists might well advocate 'anti-morality.' Writer Yukio Mishima wrote an essay with the paradoxical title *A Course in Immoral Education*. Different sets of morals for each class are referred to in order to carry out a power struggle by effectively utilizing the capital that each class possesses. In other words, morals were generated through power struggles and therefore morals in themselves are inherently superficial.

Another view incorporates the achievements of biology, arguing that the use of morals to integrate society is impossible because of social 'evolution.' The representative sociologist and exponent of this argument is Luhmann, who states that 'a society differentiated by functioning systems must relinquish moral integration' and believes that it is impossible for morals to prescribe standards of behavior in modern society (Mikami 2003). Luhmann emphasizes the lack of basis for morality in his assertion that order is established 'even without God's intervention' but places his full trust in the 'evolution' of society.

The tendency in modern social theory is therefore for a growing and common understanding surrounding the lack of basis for morality. More important, however, is the argument that morality is a tool for extracting the intention for gift-giving. Unfortunately, no mention has been made of the relationship between gift-giving and morals due to the lack of significant interest in modern sociology in the important issue of gift-giving.

Bourdieu and Luhmann also attempt to explain the lack of basis of moral values through factors which prescribe or characterize society, such as 'capital' that prescribes social behavior, the 'differentiation in functions' of society, or more simply, social 'evolution.' If, however, it were possible to explain the lack of basis for morals, such an explanation would take a non-social perspective. Morals do not exist in the state as classified in chapter 2, a state in which sociality is at a standstill or the degree-zero sociality phase. It is at this point that the lack of basis for morals becomes clear for the first time.

Moreover, it is the conman or one who is like a conman, who conveys the lack of basis of morals. The conman has no interest in what is right. The conman simply goes about persuading others by making use of whatever moral code is appropriate at a given time. It is only after the con is revealed that the discrepancy between the morals preached by the conman and his/her actions is made apparent. The victim's faith in the morals touted by the conman is betrayed as a result of the conman's actions, resulting in distrust in the morals themselves.

Although not as extreme as the conman, the ordinary person also touts and promotes morals on a regular basis in order to extract gifts and benefits. The reality is that minor but countless 'cons' are constantly being perpetuated. In order to fully maintain an organization through morals, however, other initiatives are necessary. The following instruction appears in the manual for the pyramid selling scheme mentioned earlier: 'You must first convey to the salesperson that you are enabling him/her to make money.' Although in reality it is only the owner of the company and a few sales leaders who are profiting from the scheme, the sales personnel believe that they are profiting thanks to the company. In actual fact the sales personnel are simply continuing to purchase the company's products and therefore in this sense it is the salesperson that is the gift-giver. And yet the intention is to make the salesperson believe that he/she has the opportunity to make a profit through the beneficence of the company. Morals are exploited through the establishment of a false awareness, that is, through the process of brainwashing.

However, there is always the possibility that morals can be the subject of criticism. Let us say that moral M is being utilized. There will always be someone opposed to M or who does not follow the rules of M. As a result, those who do not adhere to moral M can at times be violently punished. However, a State in which collaborativity can only be maintained through the exertion of violence, is not an ideal State. What is necessary is a system in which each person readily gives gifts so that there is no need for the exertion of violence. It is at this point that 'ancestors' are invoked.

As seen in chapter 4, Mauss points out that primordial exchange involved an exchange between the living and the dead. Before Mauss, Friedrich Nietzche also made a similar observation in *Genealogy of Morals*:

> …the living generation always acknowledged a legal obligation towards the earlier generation, and in particular towards the earliest, which

> founded the tribe (abbrev) ...There is a prevailing conviction that the tribe *exists* only because of the sacrifices and deeds of the forefathers, – and that these have to be *paid back* with sacrifices and deeds (Nietzche 1994: 65).

There is an imbalance between a sense of 'obligation' towards our ancestors, and 'us', and as a result this imbalance becomes a source of control; by demonstrating that one possesses special powers that enables communication with the gods and the spirits of the dead. This mechanism of maintaining order can be described as 'the order of recollection' in chapter 4.

The order of recollection predicates gift-giving to those in the category of the 'dead', more specifically 'ancestors', as the most important type of gift-giving, in order to absorb the intention to give gifts. If the symbolic exchange between oneself and one's ancestors is seen as the most important form of gift-giving, then any exchange with other tribes or other people would therefore be secondary. Therefore, any exchange with others (those outside the community) must be 'ratified' by the (spirits of) the dead. For example, *kula* exchange on the Trobriand Islands involves singing a song when accepting the other party involved in the exchange. The song calls on the guardian spirits of the animals to bring a necklace-like ornament via the other party involved in the *kula* exchange (Mauss 1969).

It is a ritual that attempts to symbolically convey the fact that the ornament-like gift is not from the other party but is in fact a gift from the guardian spirits.

The validity of *kula* exchange is guaranteed by a spiritual presence that exists beyond 'us.' According to market principles as represented by Adam Smith, exchange occurs spontaneously between the two parties involved in the exchange. However, in *kula* exchange, any exchange between the living is not possible without the presence of the spirits of the dead.

Transformation and gift-giving

In the way that funereal rituals are found in every society, the order of recollection is universally found wherever the dead are mourned and wherever order is maintained through exchange with the dead. However, there are always those who do not adhere to moral codes even though the assistance of ancestors or a more symbolic 'god' is called upon.

There is an alternative to the use of moral codes for extracting the intention to give gifts. This is the 'squandering' mentioned by George Bataille who was inspired by Mauss' theory (Bataille 1967). As quoted earlier, this is a concept that was born by focusing on the fact that the aim of *potlatch* is not necessarily exchange but can be 'to destroy.' The host, having given too many gifts, ends up self-destructing. In this sense, squandering represents pure gift-giving. There is an aspect to the pure intention to give a gift that is unexplainable, absurd and almost insane.

Bataille's concept of squandering can also be seen in Durkheim's 'state of agitation.' Let us take this opportunity to review Durkheim's theory.[2] Durkheim argued that religious notion is borne from agitation. He did not, however, provide a clear explanation of *how* religious notion is borne from agitation. There is a difference between a state of agitation and religious or secular morality. It is similar, however, in the sense that in the end the intention to give gifts is extracted in both. Moral codes are touted in order to extract the intention to give gifts, while a state of agitation also invites gift-giving.

As pointed out by Durkheim, agitation makes metamorphosis possible. '...everything is just as though he really were transported into a special world...and into an environment filled with exceptionally intense forces that take hold of him and metamorphose him' (Durkheim 1976: 218).

We can understand from this statement that agitation results in metamorphosis, or transformation. It is the anticipation of transformation that extracts the intention to give gifts. Durkheim saw religious notion as something that is borne from agitation because it is from this state that the intention to give gifts emerges.

I have used the term transformation from time to time, and have pointed out that someone gives money to a conman because the conman invites that person to undergo a transformation. I would now like to consider the subject of transformation in more detail (Ogino 1997a: 1–23).

There is an affinity between transformation and the term 'repetition' used by Gilles. 'Recurrence' comes to mind when one hears the term 'replication.' There is a tendency to interpret the term 'repetition' in the sense of repetition of the same act, or to continue to create the same product. However, the premise of 'repetition' here is that a certain act (or thing) has an 'identity.' Repetition is interpreted as nothing more than recurrence because repetition is seen within the context of identity. However, hidden within this recurrence is a nucleus that is not revealed outside the repetition (Deleuze 1994).

How does Deleuze view repetition? In the opening of *Difference and Repetition*, Deleuze makes the statement that 'repetition is not generality.' Something has generality if it can be exchanged or replaced by another. However, 'To repeat is to behave in a certain manner, but in relation so something unique or singular which has no equal or equivalent.'

Deleuze first cites the festival as an example of repetition. A festival represents a 'paradox' in which 'an event that can never be repeated again' is in fact repeated. This is because a festival is a ritual that repeats the beginning of the universe. It is not mere coincidence that Durkheim recognized a state of agitation in the festival. This is a clear representation of repetition that Deleuze saw as being primitive. The beginning of the world is an event like no other and in this sense can not be generalized. The festival is an irreplaceable event to the living, while for those who repeat the beginning of the world, the festival that is held each time represents a new 'beginning.'

In the way that Durkheim points out that the participants of a festival undergo a transformation, Deleuze also states that to repeat means to put on a mask and to masquerade. 'The mask is the true subject of repetition.' This can be interpreted as repetition representing transformation.

Transformation can mean that a model person exists and one attempts to become that person. There is a studio in the Gion district of Kyoto, for example, where tourists can be transformed into *maiko* [apprentice *geisha*]. A hotel that advertised the '"Pretty Woman" Transformation and Accommodation Package' attracted over 100 people. This package included 'being transformed and photographed, dinner and twin-share accommodation' for 19,800 yen ($US 170). It offered people a temporary escape from their everyday lives by checking into a hotel where they would be ushered into a specially set up room to be transformed into, for example, a prince or a princess. Also popular was an exhibition of photographs by Yasumasa Morimura of guests who had been transformed into contemporary stars such as Madonna and Michael Jackson.

Unfortunately, this temporary transformation is nothing more than an attempt to copy someone else. Madonna and Michael Jackson can undergo a real transformation, but simply copying Madonna or Michael Jackson does not represent a true transformation. For example, Madonna transforming herself for a concert represents the repetition and replication of the transformation into the unique persona that is

'Madonna.' A performer like Madonna does not need a model. This is the very repetition as argued by Deleuze.

> Repetition is truly that which disguises itself in constituting itself, that which constitutes itself only by disguising itself. It is not underneath the masks, but is formed from one mask to another, as though from one distinctive point to another, from one privileged instant to another, with and within the variations. The masks do not hide anything except other masks (Deleuze 1994: 17).

Although this text by Deleuze is difficult to understand, what Deleuze is pointing out is that stars such as Madonna and Michael Jackson are undergoing repetition as they perform, and that no model exists. A star puts on a series of masks at each concert during the performance and each 'mask' creates a 'privileged instant.' It is this very moment that represents repetition. This is what we define as transformation. What is important is that there is no 'real face' underneath the mask. Each time the star sings and dances at a concert, he/she is undergoing a new transformation into a star, and that star's performance is not based on a copycat performance.[3]

Faithfully following a model or an example during a performance or during the process of learning to perform does not constitute repetition in Deleuze's sense of the word. 'Imbalance, anxiety and asymmetry' and 'a type of rupture' are generated during the recurrence. This is what represents repetition, the effect of what we term transformation, and it is here that the difference lies.

In fact, conmen also try to create this transformative effect. Abe, for example, called himself 'an international secret service agent in pursuit of Gorgo 13', set up a company, and then, went on the run after his scam was revealed under the guise of a student sitting his University entrance exam. Abe's victim Ōbayashi , meanwhile, never knew Abe's real name. The conman mentioned in chapter 1 who told others that he was a US Air Force pilot continued to carry out his scams after making a slight name change from 'Prince Jona Kuhio' to 'Jonaf Elizabeth Kuhio.'

Frank Abagnale, the author of *Catch Me If You Can*, that was later made into a feature length film, left home at 16 and 'aged 10 years overnight' (Abagnale 1980). In other words, he passed himself off as a 26-year-old. Abagnale then carried out his scams by impersonating a jet co-pilot, a doctor and lawyer and even posed as a lecturer of sociology at one university. Moreover, Abagnale did not simply lie but actually worked in these professions, going as far as studying (which also did in his other jobs) sociology in order to be able to teach the subject

Gift-giving and collaborativity

The intention to give gifts is extracted by the power of 'ancestors' and the conman's invitation to undergo a transformation. The two appear to be completely contradictory. The former enables the reproduction of the family while the pure conman does not even consider maintaining relationships, performing as necessary at any given time. This is, however, because the order of recollection – as mentioned in this book and based on the recollection of one's ancestors – is functioning effectively.

In fact transformation is also the driving force behind the order of recollection. I have pointed out in the previous section that Deleuze saw the origin of repetition = transformation in the festival. Durkheim, too, echoing Spenser and Glen's report, emphasizes the transformation undergone by indigenous Australians during religious rituals.

> The sexes unite contrarily to the rules governing sexual relations. Men exchange wives with each other. Sometimes even incestuous unions, which in normal times are thought abominable and are severely punished, are now contracted openly and with impunity (Durkheim 1976: 216).

We do not know whether this was actually carried out, and if so, to what extent this was being carried out. What is important, however, is that transformation represents the trigger for giving gifts to the gods (reaching a peak during the offering ritual). According to Durkheim, 'a god is not merely an authority upon whom we depend; it is a force upon which our strength relies' (Durkheim 1976: 209). A god does not simply restrict. By being with god we gain confidence and are given strength.

There are numerous examples of a systematic link between transformation and gift-giving without having to travel as far as Australia. The marriage ritual in Japan in the past represents a typical ritual of transformation (Sakurai 1974). This is because the entire ritual of marriage, at the core of which lay the wedding procession, not only represents the giving of the daughter as a gift to another family, but also represents the process of transformation of the woman from the daughter into the bride/wife. In one ritual, for example, the bride must straddle a fire that has been lit outside the entrance to the house of the family into which she is marrying before she enters the house. The only other example of lighting a fire in front of the entrance to a house is when a funeral procession is departing or at the *obon* season when people welcome the spirits of the dead. The ritual of marriage is therefore in some ways similar to the ritual surrounding death. Alternatively it can be described as exemplifying the rituals surrounding death. This conveys the fact that marriage, too, represents a ritual to reproduce the order of recollection.

Order is maintained in the order of recollection through a ritualistic exchange with the ancestors. Every type of exchange is based on this model of exchange with the ancestors. Mauss cites the example of the guardian spirits being called during the *kula* exchange, on the Trobriand Islands, with those from outside the community (Mauss 1969). Not anyone can be involved in the exchange; it is only those who arrive with the guardian spirits who are received. In principle the marriage ritual is the same – the other or 'the bride' is received in the same way that the spirits of the dead are received. The spirits of the dead are not inauspicious but the spirits of the ancestors, and like the guardian spirits who guarantee the trustworthiness of the other party involved in the *kula* exchange, they too are believed to endow the community with blessings. The bride is the 'gift' brought by the spirits of the ancestors. By welcoming the bride dispatched by the spirits of the ancestors, the family undergoes a transformation.

What is evident from the above is that it is the anticipation to be transformed that promotes the intention to give gifts and it is this that also enables the reproduction of the family. Lévi-Strauss' theory on genealogy is limited because, unlike Mauss, he dismissed the perspective of primordial exchange between the living and the dead. As a result, Lévi-Strauss views marriage as a form of equivalent exchange. According to Lévi-Strauss, marriage is the result of a logical choice in 'uncivilized' society and the exchange format of marriage is established in the way that voluntary exchange takes place in Adam Smith's 'uncivilized' society. Strangely, however, Lévi-Strauss rejects the perspective of the 'reproduction' of family. Regardless, the exchange of gifts does not represent equivalent exchange. If marriage is considered to be a form of gift exchange then it should not be seen as equivalent exchange.

According to Deleuze, 'If exchange is the criterion of generality, theft (*vol*) (Author's note: this is not *dol* that appears in 'Preface' but *vol*. It is a term often used to signify misappropriation but can also mean 'fraud' and I believe that in Deleuze's sentence it is appropriate to translate this term as 'fraud') and gift are those of repetition' (Deleuze 1994: 1). 'Exchange' as used by Deleuze assumes that there is equivalence between two objects. In contrast, the exchange of gifts does not represent equivalent exchange. Moreover, there is no intention to realize equivalent exchange in pure gift-giving (gift-giving that does not produce a cycle of exchange). Acts of fraud that extract the intention to give a gift are naturally also the opposite of equivalent exchange.

This, however, does not mean that equivalent exchange based on market principle, and scams and gift-giving should be viewed as complete opposites. Certainly, organizations such as corporations and banks appear to be complying with the ethics of market economics. As a result such organizations seem to hold a view of justice that exchange should be equivalent. In reality, however, corporations do not necessarily behave in conformance with market economics. At times corporations comply not with the theory of market economics but with the theory of gift-giving. International Union Development Center, the company set up by Abe, was a strange company that complied with the theory of gift-giving. There is, however, a general tendency for corporate organizations to be drawn into scams. The late 80's in Japan was called the era of the bubble economy, and we are all aware of the fact that during this time the banks generously financed projects without knowing whether the loans would be repaid and, as a result, found themselves with enormous amounts of bad debt. The attitude of the banks during this time was essentially no different from that of Abe. It would in fact be more appropriate to say this attitude was no different from that of Ōbayashi , the loan officer at the Ashikaga Bank. The banks were lending money indiscriminately to its customers during the bubble economy, in the same way that Ōbayashi lent/gave the bank's funds to Abe. The banks continued to finance projects – under the illusion that they would eventually see a profit – or, more to the point, automatically provided finance even though it was unclear whether the funds would ever be repaid.

Alternatively, like the IT millionaires of Silicon Valley, not only are profits demanded but there is also a desire to become involved in 'volunteering', 'donating', and 'philanthropy', in order to convey their intention to give. This intention to give gifts is not completely unrelated to market principle and indeed, market principle may not be able to exist without the intention to give gifts. In this sense, arguably the theory that binds gift-giving and fraud – rather than the market economy – is what is fundamental.

The intention to give gifts in itself does not represent a social characteristic. The intention to give gifts amongst sympathizers wanting to give money to conmen is not part of a social movement. In fact, there is a tendency to establish a secret world, a world of degree-zero sociality that outsiders can neither see into nor know. It is, however, from this world of degree-zero sociality that an ongoing collaborativity emerges. In other words, collaborativity can be established without physical violence (disasters), or violence exerted in an attempt to control others.

An example of this is the illegally occupied District M, an area of 34,000 square meters that lies within the grounds of Osaka Airport beside one of its runways, which is currently being researched by Kiyoshi Kanebishi (Kanebishi 2001).

District M is the site of the boarding facilities that housed the Korean laborers working on the extension to the airport in the years before World War II. The US military requisitioned the airport after World War II and used it for some years but did not evict the residents. Eventually District M was established. The dwellings were crude, often built of plywood and other materials, and fires were frequent (Kanebishi 2001: 424). District M was a degree-zero sociality area. However, the understanding amongst its residents was that it was a place where 'anyone who is poor, whether they are South Koreans, North Koreans or Japanese can come to' and every resident felt a degree of comfort living here.

However, the community found itself facing a major issue – the problem of waste disposal.

> Before 1971, the owner of a vacuum truck who lived in the district took it upon himself to carry out the waste disposal in the district. He collected a fee from the residents and then disposed of the waste at the City's sanitation department. However, the ability for the City to process the waste reached its limits and the City in the end rejected any waste from unregistered and illegal businesses. The waste and rubbish was therefore no longer removed from the district, becoming a problem for the district's residents (Kanebishi 2001: 421).

It was at this time that Mr F stood up to solve the problem of the odor in the district resulting from the accumulating waste. F formed a residents' association and lobbied the City for the latrine waste to be collected. Once this matter was solved, he then lobbied the City for the streets to be paved. The City's attitude was that it had no obligation to look after residents who chose to illegally occupy the site. Even the district's residents were derisive of F, believing that his efforts were a waste of time. Despite the prevailing attitude, F spent around 500 days over a period of three years carrying out a 'sit-in' at City Hall. Eventually the paving was approved. F's argument during this time represents a paradoxical argument – what he was trying to do was not impossible because it was illegal but in fact was possible even if it was illegal.

Something is only 'illegal' within the context of the laws of the time. Something may not in fact be 'illegal' within the context of fundamental justice that predates current law. If the above situation is viewed from the perspective of whether the minimum degree of life is being guaranteed, then arguably a situation in which waste is not being processed, and there is no water supply, sewerage system or phone, should never be permitted. It is, however, not an easy thing to arrive at the awareness that justice can be demanded of the government within an illegal context, and even more difficult to actually produce results. F was regarded by his fellow residents as a Don Quixote-like figure who was attempting something impossible. Moreover, because of the time he spent lobbying the government, he was clearly unable to commit himself either to work or family.

F represents someone who faithfully adheres to the principle of pure gift-giving. F first moved into this illegally occupied district because a man who claimed to have been the vice-commander of the battleship Yamato appeared before him one day and asked him for a donation to build a memorial at the foot of Mt Fuji to honor those who had died on the battleship. F gave this man all the money he had. The district's residents were apparently also aware of F's strong intention to give. Take the following example. One day F's wife complained to an elderly woman living in the district that F was obsessed with the activities of the residents' association and was neglecting his family. The elderly woman then got up from her seat, walked out and soon returned with a bundle of notes – around two million yen ($US 17,000) – and persuaded F's wife to take the money (Kanebishi 2005: 74).

There are no clear rules in a district that is out of the loop of the restoration that is carried out immediately after a disaster or war. The result is a situation in which it is unclear as to what exactly constitutes 'validity.' From such a situation emerge those who do not doubt the validity of self-assertiveness. For them, their belief in their own validity lends itself to the validity of self-assertiveness. These are people who see validity in the belief in their own validity. I shall call this sort of justification 'self-fulfilling justice.'

The concept of self-fulfilling justice is similar to Hayek's self-organization and systems theory described in chapter 3. The grounds for justice can not be explained, in the same way that Baba argues that a system is nothing more than 'an empty ring' that can not claim any grounds for its existence. What is interesting, however, is that there is still the possibility for self-fulfilling justice to give rise to a sense of public duty. Once the majority's consent is obtained, its benefits can then provided. Indeed, not every self-fulfilling justice is recognized as being valid. There are conditions for a self-fulfilling justice to become community based, and they are as follows:

1. A sense of community must be initiated by the parties involved.
2. Only problems that can not be solved through self-reliant efforts are to be addressed. Therefore, statements attracting criticism of self-interest can not be made.
3. The benefits for 'the forgotten people' and 'people who don't assert themselves' must be considered.

If these conditions are fulfilled, then self-fulfilling justice can take on the characteristics of a community (Ogino 1999: 343–4). The intention to give gifts is extracted when each of these conditions are realized.

In such a situation, the intention to give gifts does not look to 'the past', such as giving gifts to one's ancestors, but looks to the future. To cite the example of the illegally occupied district, when F's wife expressed her hesitancy at accepting the two million yen that the old woman handed to her, telling her that she could never repay that much money, the old woman responded 'Pay me back some time in your life time – I don't know how long my son will live comfortably. You can return it to him when he needs it. Or when my grandchildren need it' (Kanebishi 2005: 74–5). Both 'son' and 'grandchildren' are symbols of the future, thus the gift of two million yen represents an investment in the future. Although the old woman would not be able to personally reap the profits of that investment, personal profit is of no importance to her. The act of giving is realized when a 'place' is created in which the intention to give a gift satisfies the above three conditions. The creation of such a 'place' is not necessarily the result of violence and therefore demonstrates that collaborativity is not necessarily the direct result of violence.[4]

6 The Ambiguous Other

The stranger

The aim of this book is to convey the major significance of the conman in the establishment of society. Needless to say, the definition of conman as referred to here is not restricted to malicious criminals. The focus of this book has been on the non-malicious or 'pure' conman and I have attempted to clarify the conman's hidden role in the establishment of society and, in conclusion, shall now reexamine that role.

Simmel's theory provides the first reference point in any sociological examination of 'the fraudulent individual.' As cited in chapter 1, Simmel was the first sociologist who became aware of the importance of the conman within the context of communication. He also proposed the interesting concept of 'the stranger' that can be applied to the relationship between the conman and social order (Simmel 1955).

Simmel describes the stranger as someone who is more than merely a wanderer; the stranger suddenly appears in a community and by chance remains there. The stranger is distant and yet, for some reason, so near, with whom we feel a sense of familiarity – his existence is ambiguous.

According to Simmel, this ambiguous stranger tends to appear in some places but not in others. There is almost no place for the stranger in, for example, a closed community. A community depends on a stranger for the first time when there arises a need to obtain goods from outside the community. Hence in many cases it is the merchant who is the first stranger to appear within a community.

If so, how do the members of the community view the stranger as represented by the merchant? A characteristic of the stranger is that he/she is not related or close to anyone in the community and therefore is able to conduct oneself as if he/she occupied an 'objective existence.' It is an ambiguous type of behavior in which the stranger 'is distant yet close; is disinterested and yet can, at times, actively participate.' This gives the stranger a unique status and appears to offer others a sense of 'objectivity.' For example, a city in Italy used to invite judges from outside the city. Only strangers are free of vested interests; in other words, the stranger is the only person who can be truly free within that community.

The stranger, as defined by Simmel, is generally someone who has a unique and valued position in the community. This does not mean, however, that the stranger is always viewed positively. The 'Jew' who appears in Edgar Morin's *La Rumeur d'Orléans* [Rumor in Orleans] is a typical stranger as defined by Simmel but is viewed negatively by the community. The Rumor is as follows.

> In May 1969 a report grew and spread through Orleans that first one, then two, and finally no less than six women's dress shops in the centre of town were running a white slave trafficking ring. Young girls were said to be drugged (by injection) while in the fitting-rooms, and then carried down to the cellars, whence they were spirited away after dark, to exotic centres of prostitution abroad (Morin 1971: 17).

There is in fact no evidence of human trafficking in Orleans. Despite this, however, the rumor gradually spread and high school students were warned 'not to enter the dress shop.' These warnings gave credibility to the rumor and eventually resulted in the students' parents gathering outside the dress shop, blocking its entrance to prevent customers from entering the store. The situation was finally resolved when the media and politicians managed to persuade the public that the rumor had no basis.

Morin investigated the ways as to how the human trafficking rumor had spread in Orleans as well as clarifying the reasons why the rumor developed. Firstly, how did the rumor begin? During the process of his investigation, Morin discovered that the source of the rumor was a female high school student. Morin sought the reason for this in the transformation undergone by the city of Orleans in recent years. There was a growing interest in the outside world amongst residents of French regional cities such as Orleans during the 1960's, as represented by an interest in fashion (the availability of ready-to-wear clothes was a catalyst for the growing fashion phenomenon) and an infatuation with things foreign. In contrast, the influence of traditional Catholic morality was weakening. Clearly, the norms that had controlled the world of Orleans in the past were disintegrating, enabling the emergence of a situation in which sociality almost came to a standstill.

The owner of the dress shop who had introduced consumer culture into Orleans became a target of criticism. He represented the merchant-stranger who came from outside Orleans to open a store in the town. Although he appeared to be a respectable citizen, those who believed the rumor were distrustful, suspecting him of having links with the threatening world that lay beyond the city. Indeed, the shop's quick expansion added veracity to the rumor. According to the rumor, the dress shop had expanded with the profits of human trafficking.

Unlike the judge in the Italian city, the dress shop owner is not seen as being objective: he is someone to be rejected, a scapegoat. This indicates that there are several different dimensions to the ambiguous position of the stranger. On the first level of ambiguity, the following differing dimensions can be found: the stranger's actions can alter depending on the situation; the stranger can either be disinterested, or become an active participant, in that situation; or furthermore, the stranger can appear (in the eyes of those in the community) to undergo a change. On this level, ambiguity is generated by the fact that the distance between the stranger and the community can be altered depending on the situation.

On the second level, the ambiguity is related to the way the stranger is evaluated. This can mean that the stranger appears to be an objective or free person. This is because the difference in the degree of willingness displayed by the stranger, depending on the situation, is viewed as being determined by how the stranger will personally benefit. In this way, the objectivity or freedom of the stranger can at times be viewed positively, while at other times the stranger can be deemed a threat, prompting an (unnecessary) change within the community. This latter level of ambiguity applies to the example of the dress shop owner in Orleans who became the target of negative rumors.

Having confirmed that there are two different dimensions to this ambiguity, let us now define the ambiguity of the stranger as 'the ambiguity of the other.' The reason for the use of the more neutral term 'the other' rather than the term 'the stranger' is that the latter term can have a negative connotation. The use of 'the other' avoids any misunderstanding. In fact, through the history of sociology, Simmel's 'stranger' has been dwarfed by social categories such as 'the outsider' who does not assimilate mainstream norms or the 'marginal man' who represents social minorities such as migrants.[1] 'The outsider' is also a term indicating those living outside the community and that the term does not incorporate an aspect of involvement, on some level, with the community is another reason why the term 'the other' is used here.

Nevertheless, the term 'the other' used in this context is not the same as 'the other' used in the context of 'the other' versus 'the self.' Let us now examine the other's place inside and outside the community or amongst multiple communities.

The ambiguous other

Normally, in everyday language, the statement 'Belongs to A or B' means that if one belongs to society A, then one does not belong to Society B. Returning to the example of 'Rumor in Orleans', the citizens of Orleans are those born and raised in Orleans. Those who are not Orleans citizens therefore do not belong to Orleans.

In contrast, 'the other' is involved in two different societies – Society A and Society B. The Orleans dress shop owner is viewed as being related to both A (Orleans) and B (outside Orleans = a distant country). The owner can be described as being 'related to A and B.' Needless to say, it is logically possible to 'belong to A and B' and 'belong to A or B.' However, the condition of existence of 'belonging to A or B' is measured by a different logic from that of the existence of 'belonging to A and B', and for a long time, it was thought that applying the same logic to these two conditions of existence was not possible.

However, in symbolic logic developed in the 19th Century, the same logical formula was applied. This is because there was a change in the definition of the logical formula 'A or B.' Logic predating symbolic logic defined it as how it was defined in everyday language; it was something that was not inherited by symbolic logic. How, then, is 'A or B' defined in symbolic logic?

The 'OR' in symbolic logic has three ways of being true. Firstly, something belongs to A but does not belong to B. Secondly, something belongs to B but does not belong to A. These two are the same as the 'or' in everyday language. However, the 'OR' in symbolic logic also incorporates the situation in which one 'belongs to A and B.' Therefore, not only those belonging to A or B, but those belonging to both A and B can be expressed as 'OR.' Both 'belonging to Orleans' and 'belonging outside Orleans' can be described in the formula 'A or B.'

The definition of 'OR' prior to symbolic logic (in which 'A and B' was not included) is referred to as an 'exclusive disjunction' or XOR. In contrast, 'OR' in symbolic logic is referred to as an 'inclusive disjunction', or simply as a 'disjunction.'

This transformation in the definition of 'OR' in logic is also of great benefit in sociology. This is because the two logics of 'exclusion' and 'inclusion' also represent the logic of the establishment of society. Defining 'OR' as an exclusive 'OR' excludes others who do not completely belong to the community. This is because only those belonging to a community are 'true' and those who do not are 'false.' In this case, someone belonging to multiple collectives is not tolerated. Let us call the logic that promotes exclusion in this way 'the logic of exclusion.'

In a feudal society, for example, everyone including feudal lords belonged to a manor or dominion. If one belonged to Manor A, one was not permitted to belong to Manor B. In other words, one belonged to either Manor A 'OR' Manor B and could not belong to both. Some, such as merchants and artists, moved from Manor A to Manor B, but if one followed the logic of the manor these individuals would not be recognized as members of society. Obviously, wanderers in feudal society were not totally rejected. The wanderer, however, represents a logic that is different from that of the settled residents belonging to the manor. Because the wanderer moves between multiple manors, we can say that he/she represents logic 'A and B' (connected to Manor A and Manor B). Alternatively, as he/she does not belong to A or B, the wanderer can, in contrast, be seen as 'not being' residents of A and 'not being' residents of B, that is, 'Not A' and 'Not B.' According to the logic of exclusive disjunction, 'OR' applies to neither. This can be expressed by a simple logical operator which I shall omit. However, what is of importance here regardless is that wanderers and the settled residents who belonged to a manor were perceived as belonging to completely different modes of existence and logic.

Underpinning the manor is the order of recollection established through the symbolic exchange that takes place between the ancestors and the community. This does not, in principle, recognize others from outside the community. However, this is only in principle. If we recall Tsuneichi Miyamoto's Genji of Tosa, it is evident that wanderers are not always rejected immediately. If anything, the village looks after the beggar Genji of Tosa. In this example Genji of Tosa is seen as being closest to God, and therefore offering him support is perceived as essentially the same as the same making offerings to God.

In other words, a community sustained by the order of recollection as a rule rejects 'the other.' If 'the other' is accepted into a community, it is based on an understanding that 'the other' is involved in some way in the community. There is therefore no equality in the relationship between 'the other' and the members of a community. 'The other' is either viewed positively as being close to God and accepted into the community, or his/her presence is negated and rejected.

As in the judge in the Italian city described by Simmel, at times 'the other' can play an important role in the establishment of society. 'The other' can also, however, be subject to rejection. The scapegoat in chapter 4 is a typical example. Those who are scapegoated are, for example, wanderers who have no direct connection with the village. However, this does not necessarily mean that anyone who is not a farmer always ends up being a scapegoat. The violent device that creates a scapegoat operates when crisis strikes a village or town. The Rumor in Orleans coincided with a time of massive upheaval for the city of Orleans. There is an awareness that violence must be exerted towards others for order to be restored.

However, the dress shop owner who became the subject of rumors in Orleans and almost ended up becoming a scapegoat was, in the end, rescued by the media and politicians. By rejecting the other (=exerting violence), the citizens of Orleans in the end rejected the XOR logic to restore order. In addition to the condition of existence represented by the everyday language 'OR (exclusive disjunction)' – 'Belongs to Orleans and does not belong outside Orleans' and 'Belongs outside Orleans and does not belong in Orleans' – that is determined as being 'true', there is also a world in which the condition of existence represented by the statement 'belongs to Orleans and outside Orleans' can also be 'true.' Whether one belongs to a specific group or belongs to multiple groups is not the issue. Both are seen as being 'true.' This is the world bound by the logical formula (disjunction) 'OR' in symbolic logic.

This is a world different from that governed by the order of recollection. This is because the issue of whether one belongs to one or multiple organizations is not determined by a separate logic but controlled by the same logic (disjunction). According to this logic, there is no preoccupation with whether one claims loyalty to one organization or belongs to multiple organizations. If anything, it is logical to recognize both. Let us call this logic 'the logic of inclusion.'

Let us now return to the issue of the ambiguity of 'the other.' I have already pointed out that the ambiguity of the other has two dimensions. One is the ambiguity in the sense of either a positive or negative evaluation of 'the other.' Ambiguity in this sense of the word is generated when an exclusive logic operates, the principle of which is that one belongs to a specific community. This is the logic of a society that fears the exposure of 'the other', and there is only one choice to be made – either to reject 'the other' or to positively evaluate him/her as someone exceptional (God-like) and to incorporate that person into the community. 'The other' is therefore either rejected or elevated to an exceptional status and in a strict sense, therefore, 'the other' does not exist.

In contrast, the ambiguity – in the sense of a change in distance between 'the other' and the organization – is not revealed when the logic of exclusion is dominant. If belonging to a certain organization is obligatory, then changing the distance between that person and the organization is not, as a rule, permitted. A stranger takes on the role of a judge in the Italian city because the citizens have a duty to serve their city.

Symbolic logic and market economics

Symbolic logic was developed by De Morgan and Boule in England during the 19th Century. Until then, 'Since its dramatic emergence in ancient Greece, no essential development took place in logic for around 2,000 years' (Komatsu 197: 11). It was probably not mere coincidence that a new development in logic took place at the beginning of the 19th Century. Symbolic logic expressed the state of affairs which was to follow from this new development. In this world, one was able to belong to a single world and yet be involved in multiple worlds. This is the world into which market economics penetrated.

The world into which market economics penetrated is – to quote Adam Smith, who advocated market economics during 18th Century England – 'a world in which anyone can be a merchant.' Something has value as a 'product' in the world to which the purchaser belongs because that thing is scarce. This therefore necessitates the exchange between 'the stranger', or in other words, between those who belong to different groups. Everyone must deal with each other as 'others.' It is when this happens that, for the first time, an exchange between 'individuals' takes place. As pointed out by Louis Dumont[2], the individual is someone who is recognized as autonomous, in other words one who is free and who does not completely belong to society. This is, like the judge in the Italian city, an individual who is able to easily distance himself from the organization. Arguably, therefore, this is an individual who can, as far as possible, be defined as 'the other.' He is someone who is constantly being urged to leave the organization to which he belongs and to have contact with 'others' by becoming 'the other.' In this sense, the individual is an ambiguous 'other' who is actively involved with the outside world as someone who can make autonomous decisions. I would like to stress that this does not mean that the individual necessarily recognizes that he/she belongs to two different worlds, and, as analyzed by Yoshiyuki Yama, in fact has a strong sense of self-awareness. If the boundary between what lies within oneself and external to oneself is not clear (the division of worlds) then one is unable to recognize the existence of a different world. On an individual level, however, there is a strong sense of being trapped in the self-awareness called 'I' (Yama 1996). Western social theory, obsessed with this type of self-awareness, the premise of which is a separation of 'worlds', is different from the world of symbolic logic. The former is underpinned by a logic based on a clear contrasting of, or confrontation between, A and B, with an inability to recognize the ambiguity of 'the other.'

Incidentally, in reality, the implied world of the autonomous individual does not always emerge immediately. To those that recognize 'the other' as such, 'the other' is a maverick presence. 'The other' explains this as 'difference.' Difference is not something that is socially recognized immediately. Difference is only recognized when it is socially identified. Difference can only become valid within the context of identity. Difference that is not absorbed by identity – 'the other' – is rejected. This has been made possible through ancestors and god. Even if one belonged to a different class and therefore would not, under normal circumstances, be permitted to speak with or even look upon the face of someone belonging to another class, the community is maintained by these different classes simply because there is a recognition that both worship the same god. It is god that allocated position, status or class to people and most never doubted how things were.

As represented by the 'untouchables' in the Indian caste system, for example, people who belong to the lowest caste in a community do not represent 'others.' This is because the untouchables have their own place – although perverted – in this society. The same applies to social categories such as 'the outsider' who does not assimilate mainstream norms, or the 'marginal man' who represents social minorities such as migrants.

However, both the Brahmins (the highest caste) and the untouchables perceive each other as being similar to 'the other' and indeed can be defined as 'others.' This is because the two opposite castes are seen by each other as being absolutely different from each other, with only 'silence' apparently existing between the two (Dumont 1966). If one caste is seen as representing identity, then the other caste is seen as representing difference. No equal exchange takes place between those belonging to different castes. Asymmetrical relationships form the very foundation of caste society.

The differentiation (discrimination) between castes becomes possible with norms that convey this discrimination. The fundamental standard on which norms are based is whether a certain act is recognized as unclean or not. For example, the strict observation of vegetarianism by a caste means that that caste has a very low level of uncleanliness, making it superior to a caste that does not strictly observe vegetarianism. To claim vegetarianism simply represents an announcement of sharing a common bond with all castes that follow vegetarianism. It is also a statement that differentiates one's caste from castes that do not follow vegetarianism. Similarly, permitting a widower to remarry signifies uncleanliness, and therefore castes are then divided further depending on whether this can be permitted or not.

The concept of 'uncleanliness' – the principle that differentiates the castes – is, however, shared by all castes. No caste questions this shared principle and it is because of this that the caste system has been maintained as a valid system. In other words, those who belong to different castes belong to the same world in the sense that all follow the same principle. The only differences between castes are differences within this context and are therefore only 'secondary' differences. In other words, these differences are the representations of 'the other' or the image of 'the other.' In order for the statement 'You must not have any contact with the social category A because A is inferior to us' to be valid, a clear image of A, 'the other', must be cultivated.

The representation of 'the other' dispels the anxiety and the sense of the unknown that 'the other' creates. The caste system arguably represents the most complete manifestation of a system based on the premise of the 'inequality' of differentiated social categories. In the order of recollection, 'the other' is accepted based on the understanding that 'the other' has a relationship with the community's God. In the caste system, however, this logic is utilized to determine the social category of a caste by the distance between the caste and God. The Brahmins, who are closest to God, are positioned at the top, while the untouchables are the furthest from God. In the order of recollection, a logic operates in the face of crisis whereby someone who is seen to be 'the other' is rejected. In the caste system, 'the other' is not completely eliminated like the scapegoat. Instead, even those who are farthest from god are given a place in the world. They are thus slowly 'destroyed.' In this sense, the untouchables are scapegoats who were not killed.[3]

As a system, the caste system builds a closed and contained world. It is a system which Weber described as 'demiurgy.' In this system, craftsmen live in the village and rcceive a share of the land or the harvest instead of working for no pay (Weber 1924). There is no possibility of a market economy developing in such a system, and consequently there is little possibility of the merchant appearing in the community as 'the other.'

In contrast, 'the other' is recognized as such in a world into which market logic has penetrated. This is a world bound by an inclusive logic that makes it possible for one to belong to multiple worlds. This is only possible when 'the other' that exists outside the community is recognized. In order for this to happen, a clear image of 'the other' from outside the community is established. This is promoted by the merchant and currency.

Why is currency a promoter of this? This is because currency enables goods from outside the community to be obtained and in turn for one to sell the goods that one produces. It is currency that enables a change in the situation in which the world outside the community is seen as nothing more than a dark place to be avoided, to one in which a clear boundary is drawn between inside and outside the community, and yet into what allows someone belonging to a specific community to also exist outside that community. If 'the other' wants to purchase goods that can be exchanged for currency – in other words 'products' – the image of 'the other' therefore becomes established and the opacity of 'the other' can be cast aside. Currency therefore directs one's interest out beyond the community. In stark contrast to closed societies such as the caste system, there is an attempt to establish identity in two different worlds.

A world in which anyone can become a merchant does not appear immediately.[4] Currency has to be recognized by multiple communities in order for this to be realized. Moreover, as observed by Marx, a situation in which many 'others' sell their 'labor' as paid workers is necessary. This situation actually emerged, as observed by Marx himself, in England during the 19th Century. A world in which both belonging to a single world and being involved in multiple worlds is recognized is the world of capitalism in which labor becomes a product and in which paid labor permeates society.

According to market principle, paid labor represents a choice by free individuals to obtain payment for their labor in accordance with a contract. This is seen as representing equivalent exchange. Those without a product – in Marxist terms, those who do not have a means of production – sell their labor as 'individuals' for which they receive payment. Marx criticized this, claiming that workers were not receiving an equivalent in return for their labor because capitalism exploits a part of this. Therefore, the exchange between the capitalist and the worker is asymmetrical, meaning that the worker is being defrauded.[5]

Theoretically speaking, what is of importance here is not that the capitalist is evil but that the capitalist system inevitably creates exploitation. Like the worker, the capitalist is also being driven by the capitalism system.

Having said this, however, there are in actual fact countless examples of deception of workers by employers as well as examples of extensive damage to the environment and people as a result of pollution.

One example is the case of Y who was born in Honjima, Okinawa-jima in 1896 and who applied for work in Yaeyama in around 1927.

> Y was told that his job would be to cut the railway sleepers from Yaeyama to be sold to Taiwan. But when he got there he discovered that although it was within the precinct of Yaeyama, the site was in fact in a coal mine on Iriomote Island. Y got on a ferry at Ishigakijima port and after arriving at Iriomote Island he boarded a smaller boat and traveled down the river for another 30 minutes to arrive at the mine. Everybody had heard about and feared this island mine that was notorious for *yaki* (malaria).
>
> Y knew that protesting to the management that this was not what had been promised would be pointless. From the very first day, when he realized that he had been deceived, Y began planning his escape (Miki 1990: 15).

This is the story about a man who was 'deceived' and sent to a coal mine on Iriomote Island in Okinawa, but was not something that happened only in Okinawa. It is something that could have happened anywhere. A scam methodology is utilized to attract labor. Y heard that there was work cutting wood and so went to Yaeyama but the job awaiting him was nothing like what had been promised. There would have been many reasons why Y would have felt compelled to travel far distances for work, but he would not have left his birthplace if he had not believed that there was better work to be found in Yaeyama than was available in the area that he lived. Y sold his labor because he saw the potential to acquire wealth. This is how currency draws people to venture beyond the community. For a moment, the tuned-in relationship found between the conman and his sympathizer emerged between Y and the broker. Y's experience gives the impression that, without a conman, Y's labor would not have been converted into a product.

This demonstrates the importance of the role of currency. It has often been pointed out that the role of currency is to represent value. Currency enables the creation of an image of value that should be realized in the future. Alternatively, modern currency is arguably not just a means of accumulating wealth (an expression of value that was realized in the past), but has been created as a representation of wealth that should be realized in the future. The words 'be realized in the future' means that the individual is able to build wealth. It is often believed that this takes place in a world different from that to which one belongs. In this sense, currency projects the concept of time, called 'the future', onto a physical place. The issue lies in the fact that the value of the future is indeterminate and that value is not necessarily realized as it is anticipated. There is also a link between this reality and the occurrence of fraud and scams.

Gambling and risk

Currency enables the exchange of products between individuals and at the same time is also used to buy and sell the distinctive product called 'labor.' As pointed out in chapter 1, due to the difference in the level of knowledge between the vendor and the purchaser, there is a possibility of fraud and scams during the process of buying and selling between individuals. Even in the absence of this possibility, the purchaser (the consumer) is often dissatisfied (Hirschman 1982).

Matters become even more complicated when an exchange of labor products takes place. At times the vendor (of labor) is deceived, as in the example of Mr Y's, while at other times the purchaser loses out. Loss on the part of the purchaser often took place during the preparatory stage of capitalism, in particular. A typical example is that of a junior clerk running off with the store's cash during the Edo Period. It was the pocketing of funds by the cashier of a bank that resulted in the development of legislation against fraud in England, and in this sense, this example is no different from the Ashikaga

Bank Embezzlement described in this book. It is clear, however, that in many cases the purchaser is in a superior position in the purchase and sale of labor.

Furthermore, as typically seen in issues related to environmental pollution, there are corporations that pollute the environment surrounding the plant or the residents living there, in order to increase profits and yet do not acknowledge what they have done. Chisso, the company that caused Minamata Disease, is a typical example. We now know that Chisso released methyl mercury, produced during the production of acetaldehyde, into the Shiranui Sea causing organic mercury poisoning. Despite this, however, Kenichi Shimada, Chisso President at the time, made the following statement in the article 'Distorted media reporting – the real face of the Minamata Disease Compensation Issue' that appeared in the December 1971 issue of *Jitsugyō no Nippon* [Business Japan]:

> We have, since October 1959, adopted a method in which waste water containing mercury is not eliminated into the sea. (Abbreviated) Therefore, the re-opening of claims for compensation[6] is akin to having an old wound reopened.

That this statement was full of falsehoods was made clear in court when it was revealed that Chisso had in fact been releasing contaminated water into the ocean until the production of acetaldehyde was terminated with the announcement of the government's official position in 1968[7]. Chisso then went on to distribute a booklet titled *Minamatabyō mondai no jūgonen* (*15 years of the Minamata disease issue*) amongst its employees in 1972, in which it was claimed that the cause of Minamata disease was not plant waste but probably due to agricultural chemicals. The Minamata disease lawsuit verdict was finally announced in 1973, resulting in victory for the patients, who were the plaintiffs, and as a result direct negotiations began between President Shimada and the patients at Chisso's Tokyo headquarters. Even during the negotiations, Shimada who initially stated that he wanted to 'offer his deepest apologies' soon after claimed that 'The company's finances have been stretched to the limit because of the growing number of patients and we are in a lot of trouble if this means that we can't even pay compensation to the earlier cases' and attempted to change the agreement to suit Chisso (Ishimure 1974).

When discussing capitalist 'fraud', the issue is not simply 'exploitation' of the workers employed by the capitalist. In the case of

Minamata disease, for example, Chisso, knowing that it was causing significant damage to the environment and the residents living near the factory and that the waste water it was releasing into the ocean was causing the pollution, continued to conceal this fact. It was perpetrating fraud against even fishermen who were not directly involved with the company.

Fraud is inevitable in a capitalist society. This is because 'risk' is a premise of the capitalist system. People are constantly induced to travel beyond the world to which they belong. Although a characteristic of this system is that it enables people to transcend the boundary separating the world in which they live from the external world, the consequences are unpredictable. The external world is always unclear and yet it is this risk that makes capitalism possible. From entrepreneurs and investors through to migrants in search of work – all behave in accordance with capitalism's logic of risk. Although there is no assurance that things will eventuate as anticipated, it is this gamble that represents the force that drives the capitalism system.

Others and difference

I shall now once again summarize 'the other' and 'difference' and then provide a conclusion that summarizes what the conman is.

'The other' is not something monstrous, an absolute difference that is far removed from 'convention.' Difference is first recognized when one identifies in some way with another. However, there are two ways in which difference is recognized. The first way is to confirm the difference within the sphere of influence of a certain world, specifically when there is a difference in position or status in a society or organization and that difference (and in many cases only that difference) is recognized as representing difference. 'The other' is not emphasized in this 'difference.' The second way, in contrast, is not to emphasize the fact that one exists in a closed world but rather, to affirm the transcendence of boundaries in order to move out into another world. What is recognized here is the difference that lies between two different worlds, and therefore is significantly different from the former way that 'difference' is perceived.

Within the context of the above two perceptions of 'difference', the conman makes his appearance as someone who enables another to glimpse into a world that is different from the latter example, that is, two different worlds. Certainly, the conman can lead us into a different world. The pure conman as defined in this book, however, has not established himself in a specific world. In other words, the conman does not belong to any world. It is only the conman who rejects the division of worlds, and as a result creates openings wherever he can.

As pointed out repeatedly in this book, in reality there is something 'unsocial' about the conman which indicates, clearly, that it is this that creates uncertainty. This is because the conman behaves as though every situation is unpredictable. And, the path to the future can not be established unless people gamble on uncertainty, like the conman. In fact, it is through dangerous and uncertain situations that the path to the future is established. This is because people are attracted by almost unrealizable 'stories', and these are the sort of stories that give people hope. It is only when it is uncertain whether something can be realized, when something transcends the logical and calculable ('risk' is calculable), that a story has value.

Hiroshi Shimizu theorizes about what 'the logic of place' represents through Yagyūshinkage-ryū *kenpō* (swordsmanship). Shimizu's argument is similar to that developed in this book. Needless to say, *shinken shōbu* ['fighting with real swords', playing hardball] is the premise of *kenpō.* In *shinken shōbu* one is placed in a situation in which it is impossible to predict the other's moves – what Shimizu describes as an 'all encompassing' situation. This represents, in this book, the concept of the uncertain situation. According to Shimizu, however, this is not a situation where nothing happens, nor where one acts without accordance to any rules. It is a place where *shinken shōbu* is played out, providing the swordsman with an opportunity to practice his swordsmanship, and where a story is created. The swordsman improvises, responding to the approximate plotline of the story.

During the performance, the swordsman, in order to win, moves from a situation of *jitabunri* (separation from the other) to one of *jitahibunri* (non-separation from the other). The swordsman discards his obsession with ego and adopts a perspective that allows him to see the place as one that is enabling the contest. Taking the perspective of the place is a transcendental viewpoint that simultaneously incorporates both the self and the person with whom one is fighting (Shimizu 1996). What must be remembered here is the tuned-in relationship that exists between the conman and his/her sympathizer.[8] Like the swordsman, the conman carries out an appropriate performance in accordance with the story, and he/she is in an in-tune or *jitahibunri* relationship with the other person. At this point, the conman is not obsessed by ego. This is what is meant by the conman 'gambling on superficiality'[9]. The reason the conman is able to persuade the other person is because, like the swordsman who wins in *shinken shōbu*, his skilful, improvised performance fits the story in that situation.

Fraud or *shinken shōbu* first occurs in degree-zero sociality or a situation in which sociality is at a standstill. The 'difference' conveyed by the conman at this point is different again from the two types of difference mentioned earlier. This is not difference within the context of sameness, but difference, the meaning of which Deleuze attempted to restore. This difference is extreme and excessive and in a way grotesque (and unique because of its grotesqueness), and it is the appearance of this difference that leads to identification and social recognition. As in the issue of transformation discussed in chapter 5, difference lies in the repetition of the unique/original. This is not difference in the sense of comparison with another. In order for comparison to be carried out, there must be something in common between two people that enables the comparison to be made in the first place, or in other words some kind of 'sameness.' This type of comparison, however, is negated in difference that is generated from an uncertain situation.

In reality, the pure conman's tendency is to negate the social status and role-worship that imbues people with a sense of sameness or identity. Abe, the perpetrator of the Ashikaga Bank Embezzlement, set up a company and became its president. The fact that he was able to easily win the trust of people simply by adopting the title of president demonstrates the lack of grounds for people's trust in status. Fraud exposes the fact that the very grounds of status are in fact tenuous.

The pure conman's actions do not simply open an air hole in established order. It is from the uncertainty created by the conman that social order is established. When a world with clear boundaries is viewed as 'society', a certain order results and this is maintained by a series of rules = norms. However, this is generated from an uncertain world without boundaries. Moreover, there is always the possibility that such a world can revert to a state of uncertainty. It is at this point, as Weber attempted to convey with the word 'charisma', that the need arises to behave like a conman (needless to say, the conman in this context does not necessarily have the negative connotation of a criminal). F, mentioned in chapter 5, lobbied the City in order to ensure a minimum standard of living for the residents of the illegally occupied district within the grounds of Osaka Airport, 'even if what they were doing was illegal'. It was by realizing an unrealizable story that F, like the conman, succeeded in creating a new environment for the residents.

However, because survival is the aim of the conman ('all one has to do is escape to another place and once again transform oneself'), a conman's sympathizer who refuses to attempt to survive can at times be abandoned. An example of this is the Jewish soldier Josephus described by Canetti (Canetti 1978).

Josephus fought bravely against the Roman Army but the Jews were defeated by the Romans. Josephus and other survivors hid in a cave but were discovered and urged to surrender. At that point, Josephus remembered a dream in which God told Josephus that 'tragedy will come to the Jews.' Josephus interpreted this dream as meaning that God wanted him to survive and therefore decided to 'surrender to Rome as a messenger of God.' However, Josephus' colleagues pointed their swords at him, stubbornly stating that they should choose death. Josephus realized that his colleagues were not going to change their minds and knew that it would be pointless in trying to persuade them any further. He then made a suggestion that would ensure that he, at least, would survive. He proposed a plan in which they all drew straws to decide the role of the executor. The person who drew the first straw would be executed by beheading, carried out by the person who drew the next straw. The beheading was therefore to be carried out one by one so that eventually everybody would have committed suicide. Josephus' colleagues accepted his proposal and died in succession, and somehow, it was Josephus and one other who was left. Josephus then said to the other man that he had no wish to kill him and suggested that they both surrender. The two chose to surrender to the Roman troops rather than committing suicide.

Josephus told General Vespasian, who had captured him, that he would be the next Emperor after Nero. At first Vespasian thought that Josephus was lying to ingratiate himself with the General but eventually believed Josephus and consequently protected him instead of handing him over to Nero.

Josephus was a Jewish hero and outstanding soldier and because of these qualities, and was a charismatic figure to the Jewish people. In the end, however, he betrayed his colleagues who had trusted him for his own survival. Canetti argues that Josephus probably manipulated the lottery that determined who would be killed next.

The episode in which only Josephus survived can be read as portraying Josephus as a coward who insinuated himself into Vespasianus' favour. According to Canetti, however, Josephus' example illustrates the meaning of survival. Certainly, everyone other than Josephus rejected survival and there was no way that they could have been saved. Josephus alone chose to live in the other world as represented by Rome. Josephus is someone who is in fact living in a dimension in which there is no clear division between scams and gifts, friendship and enmity. It was irrelevant to Josephus whether a decision was testament to friendship or an act of betrayal. In fact, he was an outstanding commander in war (another state of degree-zero sociality). After surrendering to the Roman troops, Josephus was eventually accepted into Roman society. Regardless of the situation he was faced with, Josephus adapted himself to that situation, moving between different worlds.

According to Canetti, this is a trait that is found in all leaders and he makes the following statement.

> The deception is complete. It is the deception of all leaders. They pretend that they will be the first to die, but, in reality, they send their people to death, so that they themselves may stay alive longer. The trick is always the same. The leader wants to survive, for with each survival he grows stronger (Canetti 1978: 241).

The sociologist and the conman

If uncertainty is found in society, then those who examine society (let us for now call these people sociologists) should view society in the same way as the conman. This is to examine a world shrouded in morality by going back to its origins – a state in which pure cons, pure imagination and pure transformation is possible. This requires a perspective that is neither neutral with an absence of subjectivity nor compliant with values that would become norms.

Taking a moral stand means that those who do not conform to a certain set of morals must be discriminated against in order for the absoluteness of those morals to be conveyed. However, if the anti-discriminatory moral code or ideology that tries to challenge the discriminatory nature of a certain morality continues to conform to the moral notion that discrimination is evil, the consequence is that those who do not follow the anti-discriminatory ideology are in turn attacked and discriminated against. Anti-discriminatory morality has the paradoxical effect of potentially creating discrimination. The sociologist, in response to this vicious cycle, would distance oneself as much as impossible from morality and ideology and search for 'a place' in which theorizing about the existence of discrimination is meaningless. Like Abe who accepted Ōbayashi with the missing finger, sociologists would then examine social relationships from a perspective that incorporates the fairness and tolerance of the pure conman. And, the ideal world from this perspective would be an integrated degree-zero ideology in which no morality or norms exist.

Notes

Chapter 1

1 According to Dumont there are two definitions of the individual. One is the individual as the smallest unit and can be called a 'solid'. The other is the individual created by modern society who is an autonomous 'moral presence' independent of society (Dumont 1977).

2 Robert Castel makes a similar point (Castel et Haroche 2001).

3 For a definition of the situation, refer to Shun Inoue who addresses 'the phenomenon of lying' in *An Approach to the Phenomenon of Lying* (Inoue 1982: 32–3), a theme similar to the theme of this book.

4 Neatly organizing the group of concepts that Goffman assumes in *Frame Analysis* would trivialize the meaning of this book. A feature of *Frame Analysis* has been to reject this type of 'manualization of knowledge'. I do not know why this major work by Goffman has not been translated into Japanese but perhaps it is difficult for academics wanting to manualize knowledge to translate a work such as this.

5 As in the 'self-presentation' concept, Goffman's works from his early to middle period can be interpreted as addressing the duality of the 'true self' and the 'performing self'. However, this is no longer evident in 'Frame Analysis' and reality is described in a unique way that flatly rejects any attempt on the part of the reader to neatly organize the apprehensions of reality.

Chapter 2

1 This is the state that Foucault called 'passion.' Refer page 14, chapter 1.

2 Goffman's concept of 'role distance' is useful in explaining this point (Goffman 1986).

3 Also of importance is the point that the decision-making generated from the degree-zero sociality phase can have a public characteristic. This will be elaborated on in chapter 4.

Chapter 3

1 Refer to chapter 4 for scapegoats.

2 Refer chapter 1, page 7.

Chapter 4

1 Refer chapter 1, Page 11.

2 The difficulty of conducting surveys of disaster victims lies in the inability to determine the actual victim population. As a result, the 'snowball extraction' sampling method and 'street interviews', in which disaster victims were found on the street, were used. The latter involved searching for disaster victims in supermarket rest areas, etc, a method similar to that used by cults to attract members.
3 Refer chapter 3, pages 47 to 48.
4 Refer chapter 2, page 35.

Chapter 5

1 *Kula* exchange is a form of exchange carried out on the Trobriand Islands and involves the exchange of necklaces and bracelets amongst a network of tribes. The necklaces are exchanged in a clockwise direction, and the bracelets in an anti-clockwise direction (Mauss 1969).
2 Refer to chapter 3.
3 The same refers to education. According to Deleuze, 'We learn nothing from those who say: "Do as I do." Our only teachers are those who tell us to "do with me", and are able to emit signs to be developed in heterogeneity rather than propose gestures for us to reproduce' (Deleuze 1994: 23).
4 Mauss's gift theory refers to a world after systems have been built. This might, according to Derrida, mean that gift-giving in itself has not been addressed. Nevertheless, the proposition that the intention to give gifts creates collaborativity represents a major discovery in sociology.

Chapter 6

1 Refer (Ogino, 1993: 300).
2 Refer chapter 1.
3 This can be interpreted as the restricted category of the untouchables being the only caste that is given the status of ambiguity. Defining the untouchables as the only caste that is not completely incorporated into the social system enables it to function as a type of 'buffering device.'
4 Refer (Ogino 1998) on the establishment of capitalism.
5 Refer chapter 5.
6 Since the release of the government's official position in 1968 (Refer Note 1), 29 households of the Patient's Families Mutual Aid Society filed a damages claim against Chisso (first compensation claim).
7 The government announced its position on Minamata disease in September 1968 and recognized that Minamata disease was the result of environmental pollution.
8 Refer chapter 1, page 11.
9 Refer chapter 1, pages 16 to 19.

Bibliography

Abagnale, Frank, 1980, *Catch Me If You Can*, Grosset & Dunlap.

Agamben, Giorgio, 1995, *Homo Sacer. I*, Giulio Einaudi Editore.

Althusser, Louis, 1970, 'Idéologie et Appareils idéologiques de l'Etat', *La Pensée*, 151: 3–38 Attribué au Baron d'Holbach, 1991, *Traité des Trois Imposteurs, Moïse, Jésus-Christ, Mahomet*, Les Editions de la passion.

Aussaresses, Paul, 2001, *Services spéciaux: Algérie*, 1955–1957, Perrin.

Baba, Yasuo, 2001, *Lūman no shakairiron (Luhmann's social theory)*, Keisō Shobō.

Bataille, Georges, 1967, *La Part maudite*, Minuit.

Bourdieu, Pierre, 1996, *The State Nobility: Elite Schools in the Field of Power,* Trans. Lauretta C. Clough, Polity Press.

Canetti, Elias, 1978, *Crowds and Power*, Trans. Carol Stewart, The Seabury Press.

Castel, Robert et Claudine Haroche, 2001. *Propriété privée, Propiété, sociale, Propriété de soi: entretiens sur la construction de l'individu moderne*, Fayard.

Chikamatsu, Monzaemon, *Sonezaki Shinjū, Meido no hikyaku, hoka gohen (Love Suicides at Sonezaki, The Courier for Hell and 5 other stories),* Yoshio Sakuda ed., 1987, Iwanami Bunko.

Clastres, Pierre, 1974, *La Société Contre l'Etat: Recherches d'anthropologie politique,* Minuit.

———, 1997, *Archéologie de la violence*, l'aube.

Davie, Maurice R, 1931, *La Guerre dans les sociétés primitives*, Payot.

Deleuze, Gilles, 1994, *Difference and Repetition*, Trans. Paul Patton, Columbia University Press.

Deleuze, Gilles, 1990, *Pourparlers : 1972–1990, Ed. de Minuit.*

Derrida, Jacques, 1992, *Given Time I, Counterfeit Money*, Trans. Peggy Kamuf, University of Chicago Press.

Descartes, Rene, 1968, *Discourse on method and the meditations*, Trans. F. E. Sutcliffe, Penguin Books.

Dumont, Louis, 1966, *Homo hierarchicus : essai sur le système des castes*, Gallimard

Dumont, Louis, 1977, *Homo Aequalis*, Gallimard.

Dupuy, Jean-Pierre et Paul Dumouchel, 1979, *L'enfer des Choses*, Seuil.

Durkheim, Emile, 1976, *The elementary forms of the religious life*, Trans. Robert Nisbet, G. Allen & Unwin.

Elias, Norbert, 1969, *Über den Prozess der Zivilisation*, Suhrkamp.

Foucault, Michel, 1994, *Dits et Ecrits IV*, Gallimard.

Foucault, Michel, 1979, *Discipline and Punish: the birth of the prison*, Trans. Alan Sheridan, Penguin.

Fujitani, Tadaaki, 1999, 'W James no junsui keiken no gainen ni tsuite – stereotaipu to kobetsusei' (The concepts of W James' pure experiences – stereotypes and individuality), *Shakaigaku hyōron* 50 (1): 75–90.

Garfinkel, Harold, 1967, "Passing and the Managed Achievement of Sex Status in an 'Intersexed' Person Part 1,"*Studies in Ethnomethodology*, New Jersey: Prentice-Hall: 116–185.

Girard, René, 1987, *Things hidden since the foundation of the world*, Trans. Stephen Bann and Michael Metteer, Athlone.

Goffman, Erving, 1961, *Encounters: Two studies in the sociology of interaction*, Bobbs-Merrill Company.

———, 1986, *Frame Analysis*, Harper & Row.

Hamada, Sumio, 2002 *'Uso' wo minuku shinrigaku – kyōjutsu no sekaikara* (*The sociology of seeing through 'lies' – from the world of statements)*, Nippon Hōsō Shuppan Kyōkai.

Hayek, Friedrich A., 1973, *Law, Legislation and Liberty, Vol. 1, Rules and Order,* Routledge & Kegan Paul.

Hirschman, Albert O., 1982, *Shifting involvements: private interest and public action*, Princeton University Press.

Hobbes, Thomas, 1985, *Leviathan*, Penguin.

Inagaki, Kyoko, 1995, 'Kyōiku, sagi, gakureki (Education, fraud and academic history)', Hiroshi Takeuchi and Hideo Tokuoka eds., *Kyōiku genshō no shakaigaku* (*The sociology of the education phenomenon*), Sekai Shisōsha: 62–78.

Inoue, Shun, 1982, 'Uso genshō e no apurōchi' (An approach to the phenomenon of lies), Shōichi Nakamura and Shun Inoue eds., *Uso no shakai shinri (Lies and social psychology),* Yūhikaku: 1–39.

———, 1999, *Asobi no shakaigaku (The sociology of play)*, Sekai Shisōsha.

Ishimure, Michiko, ed., 1974, *Ten no yamu – jitsuroku minamatabyō tōsō (The heavens are ill – records of the minamata disease struggle)*, Ashi Shobō.

James, William, 1912, *Essays in Radical Empiricism*, Longmans, Green.

Kanebishi, Kiyoshi, 2001, 'Daikibo kōkyō shisetsu ni okeru kōkyōsei to kankyō seigi – kūkō fuhō senryō chiku o megutte (Public access and environmental justice in large-scale public facilities – the illegally occupied airport district)', *Shakaigaku hyōron* 52 (3): 413–429.

———, 2005 *Ikirareta Hō*, Doctoral Thesis, Kwansei Gakuin Graduate School of Sociology and Social Work.

Katagiri, Masataka, 1996, *Puraibashii no shakaigaku – sōgo kōi, jiko, puraibashii (The sociology of privacy – mutual action, the self and privacy)*, Sekai Shisōsha.

Kawamoto, Hideo, 1991, *Autopoieshisu kaidai (Autopoiesis – a bibliographical note)*, Maturana, H.R., and Varella, F.J., Kawamoto, Hideo, trans. 'Autopoiesis – Seimei shisutemu to wa nanika (Autopoiesis and Cognition: The Realization of the Living)', 248–314, Kōkubunsha.

Kimura, Mitsue, 2000, *Sagishi no kenkyū (A study of fraud)*, Tokyo Toritsudaigaku Shuppankai.

Komatsu, Hisashi, 1997, *Kigō ronrigaku nyūmon (An introduction to symbolic logic),* Morikita Shuppan.

Komatsu, Kazuhiko, 1989, *Akureiron – ikai karano messeji (A theory of evil spirits – messages from the other world)*, Seidosha.

Lévi-Strauss, Claude, 1943, 'Guerre et commerce chez les Indiens de l'Amérique du sud,' *Renaissance*, Vol 1.

———, 1978, 'Introduction à l'oeuvre de M. Mauss,' Marcel Mauss, *Sociologie et anthropologie*, P.U.F, IX–LII.

———, 1985, *Le Totémisme aujourd'hui*, P.U.F.

———, 1962, *La Pensée sauvage*, Plon.

———, 1964, *Le Cru et le cuit*, Payot.

Lévi-Strauss, Claude, 1969, *The elementary structures of kinship*, Trans. James Harle Bell, John Richard von Sturmer and Rodney Needham (ed.), Eyre & Spottiswoode.

Locke, John, 1947, *Two Treatises of Government*, Hafner.

———, 1876, 'A Report of the Board of Trade to the Lords Justices Respecting the Relief and Employment,' Bourne, H.R. Fox ed., *The Life of John Locke*, Henry S. King & Co.: 377–391.

Luhmann, Niklas, 1995, *Social Systems,* Trans. John Bednarz and Dirk Baecker, Stanford University Press.

Mann, Thomas, 1958, *Confessions of Felix Krull, confidence man : memoirs part 1*, Trans. Denver Lindley, Penguin books.

Marx, Karl and Engels, Friedrich, 1991, *The German ideology,* Trans. C. J. Arthur, Lawrence & Wishart.

Mauss, Marcel, 1969, *The gift: forms and functions of exchange in archaic societies*, Trans. Ian Cunnison, Cohen & West.

Mauss, Marcel, 1979, *Sociology and Psychology.* Trans. Ben Brewster, Routledge and Kegan Paul.

Mikami, Tsuyoshi, 2003, *Dōtoku kaiki to modanitee – Dyurukeemu kara*

Habamasu Rūman e (*Return to morality and modernity – from Durkheim to* Habermas and Luhmann), Kōseisha Kōseikaku.

Miki, Ken, 1990, *Iriomote tankōfu monogatari* (*Tale of an Iriomote miner)*, Hirugisha.

Miyamoto,Tsuneichi, 1984, *Wasurerareta nihonjin* (*The forgotten Japanese*), Iwanami Bunko.

Morin, Edgar, 1982, *La Rumeur d'Orléans*, Seuil.

Nietzche, Friedrich, 1994, *On the genealogy of morality*, Trans. Carol Diethe, Cambridge University Press.

Nishihara, Kazuhisa, 2003, *Jiko to shakai – genshōgaku no shakairiron to <hassei shakaigaku>* (*Self and society – phenomenology and social theory and emergent sociology*), Shinsensha.

Ogino, Masahiro, 1993, 'Shakaiteki kubun no seisei to tashazō (The creation of social sectors and the image of others)', *Shakaigaku hyōron*, 44 (3): 298–313.

———, 1997a, 'Shakaigaku no henshin, henshin no shakaigaku (Transformation in sociology, the sociology of transformation)', Miyahara, Kōjirō, Ogino, Masahiro, ed., *Henshin no shakaigaku (The sociology of transformation)*, Yūhikaku: 1–23.

———, 1997b, 'Sagishi no ai, sagishi no chikara (The conman's love, the conman's powers), Miyahara, Kōjirō, Ogino, Masahiro, ed., *Henshin no shakaigaku (The sociology of transformation)*, Sekai Shisōsha: 1–23.

———, 1998, *Shihonshugi to tasha (Capitalism and the other)*, Kwansei Gakuin Daigaku Shuppankai.

———, 1999, 'Chihō jichitai to hisaisha (Local governments and disaster victims)', Iwasaki, Nobuhiko, ed., *Hinan seikatsu no shakaigaku – Hanshin Awaji daishinsai no shakaigaku 2 (The sociology of refuge life = A sociology of the Great Kansai Earthquake 2*), Shōwadō: 326–344.

———, 2001, 'Bourdou to gendaishakaigaku (Bourdieu and modern sociology)', Jōkyō Shuppan Editorial Department, ed., *Shakaigaku riron no <kanōsei> wo yomu* (*Reading the 'potential' of social theory*), Jōkyō Shuppan: 261–269.

———, ed., 2002, *Bunka isan no shakaigaku – Lūburu bijutsukan kara genbaku dōmu made* (*The Sociology of cultural heritage = from the Louvre Museum to the Hiroshima Peace Memorial*), Shinyōsha.

Pascal, Blaise, 1995 *Pensées*, Trans. A.J. Krailsheimer. London: Penguin Books.

Polanyi, Karl, 1957, *The Great Transformation*, Beacon Press.

Sahlins, Marshall, 1981, *Stone Age Economics*, Aldine Pub.

Sakurai, Tokutarō, ed., 1974, 'Foruku sōsho 3 henshin (Folklore Series 3 – Transformation)', Kōbundō.

Samuelson, Paul Anthony, 1970, *Economics,* McGraw-Hill.

Satō, Noriko, 1994, '"I" to "Yamai" no shakaishiteki kōsatsu (A social study of '"Medicine" and "Disease")', *Sociology Today,* 5: 23–33.

Sawachi, Hisae, 1976, 'Ashikaga Ginkō Jiken Zenkiroku – otoko to onna no hanzai zushiki (1), (2) (Record of the Ashikaga Bank Embezzlement – picture of a crime involving a man and a woman), *Shūkan bunshun*, Bungei Shunjū.

Schmitt, Carl, 1985, *Political theology*, Trans. George Schwab, MIT Press.

Schutz, Alfred, 1976, *Collected Papers II*, Hague: Martinus Nijhoff.

Shimizu, Hiroshi, 1996, *Seimeichi to shiteno ba no riron – Yagyūshinkage-ryū ni miru kyōsō no ri* (*Logic as knowledge of life – the logic of co-creation in the Yagyūshinkage school*), Chūkō Shinsho.

Simmel, Georg, 1908, *Soziologie: Untersuchungen uber die Formen der Vergesellschaftung*, Duncker & Humblot.

Simmel, Georg, 1955, *Conflict*, Trans, Kurt H Wolff, The Free Press.

Smith, Adam, 1986, *The Wealth of Nations,* Penguin Books.

Takeuchi, Yasuo, 2002, *Hō to seigi no keizaigaku (The economics of law and justice),* Shinchōsha.

Weber, Max, 1924, *Wirtschaftsgeschichte, Abriss der universalen Social und Wirtschaftsgeschichte*, Duncker & Humblot.

———, 1956, *Wirtschaft und Gesellschaft,* Mohr.

Yama, Yoshiyuki, 1996, 'Hanten suru kishinron – jinruigakuteki shiten to no setten (Reversal of the demon theory – contact point from an anthropological perspective)', 'Edo no Shisō (Edo Philosophy)', Editorial Committee, ed., *Edo no Shisō* 5 *(Edo Philosophy 5)*, Pelikansha: 176–191.

Yamazaki, Tetsu, Serizawa, Shunsuke, 1989, '<Ren'ai> Jiken Part 1 (Love Affair-related incidents Part 1), Shunshūsha.

Yanagida, Kunio, 1989, 'Tōno monogatari shūi (Tōno folklore collection),' *Tōno monogatari* (Tōno folklore), Kadokawa Bunko: 71–193.

———, 1990, 'Minkan Denshōron (Folklore Theory)', *Yanagida Kunio Zenshū 28 (Complete Works of Yanagida Kunio, 28)*, Chikuma Bunko: 245–506.

Index

Abagnale, Frank 70, 89
Abeles, Marc 80
affection 23–4
Agamben, Giorgio 38–9, 57
agitation 40–3, 87–8
Althusser, Louis 3
ambiguity 42, 98, 101–3, 116
  of the other 98, 101
  ambiguous figures 61
  ambiguous other 99
ancestors 42, 59, 61, 85–6, 90–1, 95, 100, 103
Ashikaga Bank Embezzlement 10, 75, 108, 111
Aussaresses, Paul 71, 72
authorities 6, 15, 67
autopoiesis 51
  autopoietic system 51–4

Baba, Yasuo 52, 95
Baron d'Holbach 49
Bataille, Georges 87
becoming possessed 80
blank spaces xii
Boule, George 102
boundaries 22, 25, 30–1, 43–4, 60, 62, 65, 67, 70, 109, 111
  between the public and the private 62, 65, 67
Bourdieu, Pierre 49–51, 83–4

Canetti, Elias 4, 42–3, 112–13
capitalism ix, 7, 77, 79, 105–7, 109, 116
  capitalist society 6, 15, 19, 49, 109
Castel, Robert 115
caste system 103–5
certainty xii, 8, 10, 21, 25, 33, 57–8, 62–3, 67–8, 70, 78, 110–11, 113
  in life 68
charisma 28–9, 40–1, 111–12
Chikamatsu, Monzaemon ix, 7
civilized 2, 3, 44, 46–7, 56, 65, 72, 74–5, 78, 82, 91
society 44, 47, 72, 82
class 6, 14, 16, 23, 47, 49, 50–1, 53, 58, 63–4, 73, 84, 103
Clastres, Pierre 44, 80, 82
collaborativity 73, 85, 90, 93, 95, 116
communication 9–10, 52–3, 74, 82, 86, 96
community 40–3, 51, 56, 60, 80, 82, 86, 91, 93, 95–107
conflict 39, 44, 46–7, 53, 57, 78, 82
conman xi, 9–54, 58, 70, 73, 75, 76, 82–90, 96, 107, 109, 110–14
  See also genuine conman, moral conman
consumer culture 98
critical theory 49, 51, 54
crowd 40, 42–3
cultural capital 84
currency 105, 107

Davie, Maurice R. 44
definition of the situation 16, 115

See also Goffman
degree-zero xii, 20–26, 39, 40, 50, 53–7, 73, 84, 93, 111–15
sociality xii, 39, 54–5, 73, 93
society xii
Deleuze, Gilles 14, 87–91, 111, 116
demiurgy 105
democracy 37
De Morgan, Augustus 102
Derrida, Jacques 75, 77, 82, 116
Descartes, Rene 8, 48
description 12, 58, 71, 73
desire for upward mobility 29–30, 83
difference 6, 9–11, 15, 17, 29–30, 32, 39–44, 50–1, 56, 69, 72–3, 81, 87–9, 98, 103–4, 107, 109, 111
distinction 4, 44, 66
Don Quixote 36–7, 94
double contingency 52
double reality 25
duality of reality 50
Dumont, Louis 4, 6, 102, 104, 115
Dumouchel, Paul 79
Durkheim, Emile 40–3, 87–8, 90

economism 44
Edda, ix, xi
either-or theory 55
Elias, Norbert 4, 42, 72
elimination 31, 33, 35, 37–8, 45–6, 48–9, 69–70, 73, 82, 105, 108
emergent order 52
emulation 32
entitification 14
equivalence 92
equivalent 2–3, 6, 8, 9, 26, 75, 77–8, 88, 91–2, 106
establishment of order 46–7, 56, 59, 61
evolution 84
exchange ix, 1–3, 6, 8, 9, 22–5, 33, 44, 57, 61–2, 74–5, 77–82, 85–92, 100, 102–7, 116
exclusive disjunction 99, 100–1
exclusivity 16, 30–1

fabrication 20
fairness 30, 114
folklore 56, 57, 80
Foucault, Michel 5–6, 14, 115
Frame Analysis 19, 28, 115
freedom 4–5, 30, 40, 47, 53, 62, 98
French Revolution 46–7

Garfinkel, Harold 17
Genji of Tosa 22–5, 57, 61, 100
genuine conman 21–2, 26, 29–32, 35
gift-giving ix, xii, 3, 26, 73–5, 77–95, 116
pure 75, 77–8, 82, 87, 92, 94
Girard, René 44–6
Goffman, Erving 17–20, 28, 115
group interviews 63

Hayek, Friedrich A. 53, 95
Hobbes, Thomas 39–40, 43, 46, 56, 65–6, 78, 82
human sacrifice 58, 61

identity 16–19, 34–8, 87, 103–5, 111
ideology 6, 31, 113
illegally occupied district 93
imagination 25, 30, 47–9, 113

Inagaki, Kyoko 50
inclusive disjunction 99
individual 3–6, 9, 14–18, 26, 40–4, 49, 54, 62–3, 68, 71–2, 78, 96, 100–3, 107, 115
individualism 1, 3–4, 8, 15–16, 69
individual interviews 63, 99, 116
Inoue, Shun 26, 115
intention to give a gift xii, 87, 92, 95
interaction 9, 10, 16, 21, 52
interviews 17, 63, 99, 116
  group 63
  individual 63
  survey 63
irony 29, 48

James, William 12
justice 2, 7–8, 30, 34, 47, 53, 59, 69–71, 92–5
  for the village 59
  in exchange 2

Kanebishi, Kiyoshi 93–4, 95
Kawamoto, Hideo 51
Komatsu, Kazuhiko 61, 102
Kōmon *See* Mito Kōmon
kula exchange 74, 86, 91

La Boetie, Etienne de 44
labor 4, 8– 9, 18, 22, 33, 77, 105–8
lack of basis for morality 84
legitimacy of control 47
Lévi-Strauss, Claude 44–5, 55–6, 74–5, 81–2, 91
live sacrifices 45
Locke, John 4, 5
logic of affinity 56
logic of place 110
Luhmann, Niklas 52, 53, 84
lynching 45–6

Mann, Thomas 10
marginal man 98, 103
market economics 3, 8, 77–8, 92, 102
market principle 2–3, 92, 106
marriage 17–18, 29, 75, 90–1
Marx, Karl 49, 77, 83, 105–6
massacre of Jews 72
Maturana, Humberto 51
Mauss, Marcel ix, xi, 3, 61, 74–5, 78–80, 85–7, 91, 116
meaning xi, 10, 12, 19, 21–2, 28, 42–3, 53, 73, 106, 111–13, 115
Minamata disease 108–9, 116
Mishima, Yukio 84
Mito Kōmon 34–9, 70
Miyamoto, Tsuneichi 7, 22–4, 33, 50, 56–7, 100
modern state 46, 62, 69–70, 72
Montaigne, Michel de 44
moral 5, 26–39, 58, 83–7, 113, 115
moral conman 30–9
morality 30–8, 41, 83–4, 87, 97, 113
Morimura, Yasumasa 88
Morin, Edgar 97
myth ix, 3, 45–6, 72, 78, 79
  of scarcity 78

natural state 39, 40, 44, 65, 82
Nietzche, Friedrich 85, 86
Nishihara, Kazuhisa 11
non-social reality 19
norms xii, 4, 5, 24–5, 30, 43, 72, 97–8, 103–4, 111–14

objectivity 51, 54, 97–8
offering ceremonies 44
Ogino, Masahiro 3, 7, 29, 36, 43, 59, 63, 87, 95, 116
order of recollection 59–62, 86, 90–1, 100–1, 104
outsiders 9, 31, 53–4, 93, 98, 103

Pascal, Blaise 47–9, 69, 83
passing 6, 17–18
past 5, 14–25, 42, 90, 95, 97, 107
performance 10–11, 32, 89, 110
Polanyi, Karl 3
poor 5, 40, 93
potlach 79
premise of the economics 78
products 3, 6, 8–9, 15, 21, 49, 77–8, 83, 85, 87, 105–7
property 4–5, 75, 78
psychologism 14
pure experience 12
pure gift-giving *See* gift-giving

questionnaire survey 31, 63

reason ix, 1, 2, 5, 12, 15, 23, 25, 28, 34–7, 48, 52, 58, 68, 96–8, 110
record 5, 21, 69, 76
repetition 87–92, 111
reproduction 90–1
resume 21
revolution 41–6
risk 33, 74, 81, 107–10
role 2, 22, 25, 29, 41, 49–51, 70, 75, 82, 96, 101–2, 107, 111–12, 115
Rumor in Orleans 97, 99, 101

Sahlins, Marshall 78
Samuelson, Paul Anthony 78–9
scams ix–x, xii, 6–11, 26, 89, 92, 107, 113
scapegoats 57, 59, 61, 98, 101, 105, 115
scarcity 78–9
Schmitt, Carl 38
Schutz, Alfred 11, 36
segmentalization of the world 54
sekenshi 24, 57
self-fulfilling justice 95
self-organization 53–4, 95
self-presentation 17, 115
self-reliance 68
sense of order 36–7
Shimizu, Hiroshi 110
shut-down of sociality 39
Simmel, Georg 9–10, 44, 96–8, 101
Smith, Adam 2–4, 86, 91, 102
social force 41–2
social order 39, 40, 44–6, 53, 59, 96, 111
social policy 43
social status 23, 26, 43, 111
social system 52, 53, 116
society's violence *See* violence
solicitation 31, 32
Sonezaki Shinjū ix, 7
spectators 31–7
squandering 87
state of agitation *See* agitation
state of exception 38
state of war *See* war
strangers 7, 31, 37, 74–5, 81, 97
strategies to create distance 32
superficiality 18, 20, 110
symbolic interaction theory 16
symbolic logic 99, 101–3

symbolic violence *See* violence
system of discipline 5
system theory 51–2

theory of confrontation 55
Tōno monogatari 57–61, 72
totalitarian 37
transcendental perspective 51
transformation 14, 30, 34–6,
  66, 87–91, 97, 99, 111–13
tricks of power 37
tuned-in relationship 21, 31, 53,
  56, 81, 107, 110

uncertainty 57–8, 62, 68,
  110–11
uncivilized society 44

validation of authority 37
Varela, Francisco 51
violence xii, 25, 31, 35, 38–62,
  65, 70–2, 79, 80–2, 85, 93,
  95, 101
  symbolic 25, 39, 50, 82
  society's 39, 43, 44, 51
violent person 82
volunteer 66, 80, 92

wanderer 96, 100–1
war 2, 44, 81–2, 113
  state of 39–40, 82
Weber, Max 28, 40, 105, 111

Yama, Yoshiyuki 10, 94, 103
Yanagida, Kunio 56–61